Practical Strategic Management

How to Apply Strategic Thinking in Business

Eiichi "Eric" Kasahara

Rikkyo University, Japan

 **World Scientific**

NEW JERSEY · LONDON · SINGAPORE · BEIJING · SHANGHAI · HONG KONG · TAIPEI · CHENNAI

Published by

World Scientific Publishing Co. Pte. Ltd.

5 Toh Tuck Link, Singapore 596224

USA office: 27 Warren Street, Suite 401-402, Hackensack, NJ 07601

UK office: 57 Shelton Street, Covent Garden, London WC2H 9HE

Library of Congress Cataloging-in-Publication Data
Kasahara, Eiichi, 1958–
     Practical strategic management : how to apply strategic thinking in business / Eiichi Kasahara,
Rikkyo University, Japan.
       pages cm
     Includes bibliographical references and index.
     ISBN 978-9814641555 (hardcover : alk. paper) -- ISBN 9814641553 (hardcover : alk. paper) --
ISBN 978-9814651363 (softcover) -- ISBN 9814651362 (softcover)
     1. Strategic planning. 2. Industrial management. I. Title.
     HD30.28.K367 2015
     658.4'012--dc23
                                      2014041298

British Library Cataloguing-in-Publication Data
A catalogue record for this book is available from the British Library.

In-house Editor: Philly Lim

Typeset by Stallion Press
Email: enquiries@stallionpress.com

Printed in Singapore

Acknowledgements

This book benefited substantially from real-world business experience gained over the years from hundreds of business practitioners. I appreciate what I learned from my consulting clients in high-tech, electronics, automobiles and other industrial organizations and institutions. I express my gratitude to executive seminar participants at universities, and academic and trade conferences. I also would like to thank the students at Saint Paul's/Rikkyo University, who provided important input and feedback. I am also indebted to Dr. Kashiwagi, Dr. Shimaguchi, Dr. Michael Hutt, Mr. Charles Cohon, Dr. Obayashi, Mr. Hisada, Mr Usui, Professor Fukuda, Professor M. Sarvary, Dr. Kamekawa, and Dr. H. Schutte for their great support and keen suggestions from both practical and academic viewpoints. I also would like to thank the talented staff of World Scientific Publishing. In particular, Ms. Philly Lim provided valuable and useful advice for the book. Last, but not least, I specifically thank you for reading *Practical Strategic Management: How to Apply Strategic Thinking in Business*!

About the Author

Eiichi "Eric" Kasahara is an associate professor of marketing at Saint Paul's/Rikkyo University Graduate School of Business Design, Tokyo, Japan. He also serves as the president of the Asia Pacific Research Institute of Marketing (APRIM), and is a visiting scholar at the Technology Management School of the Shibaura Institute of Technology, Tokyo.

Personal history

Dr. Kasahara earned his Ph.D. from the International Studies Program of the Waseda University Graduate School (International Management), and his MIM from the Thunderbird School of Global Management. He subsequently worked as a fund manager for Japanese and American institutional investors. Dr. Kasahara joined the Fuji Research Institute Corporation (currently Mizuho Research Institute Ltd.) in 1989, providing consultation at the Marketing Strategy/Kasahara Cluster. He later held the post of professor at the Saint Paul's/Rikkyo University Graduate School of Business Design. Dr. Kasahara currently conducts graduate school research and educational activities. He also consults at the Asia Pacific Research Institute of Marketing on cross-functional problem-solving support for blue chip companies and SMEs, and on growing medium sized business clients in areas ranging from R&D and business development to marketing, sales, finance (IPO, M&A), corporate communication (CI, IR), executive training, and so on.

Research activities

Dr. Kasahara is presently conducting joint research on strategy and marketing with researchers from the USA, Israel, Italy, and Singapore. He is also implementing many action-based learning projects in Singapore, Hong Kong, New Delhi, and Kuala Lumpur. His research applies theories and concepts related to B2B marketing, strategic management, consumer behavior, marketing management, marketing research, global marketing, venture management, and other fields.

Preface

I have been blessed with many opportunities to be a part of stimulating consulting projects with different corporations. Giving lectures or conducting research at the graduate level are, of course, very thought provoking too; but as consulting is "an opportunity to practice theory," it is very exciting. Normally, once the strategy formulation process is complete, the client team takes the lead to actively implement the execution process. At that point, I often provide lectures on strategic management or strategic marketing to the team leaders or staff members who are in charge of implementation. In such cases, as much as possible, I try to avoid theories that are excessively detailed, and conversely, an analysis that is too broad. Why? The answer is simple: these subject matters are completely useless when making strategic judgments on a business level.

There is already a great deal of literature on management. These include many theoretical books that analyze subjects ranging from strategic management to competitive strategy, strategic marketing, marketing management, consumer behavior, management of technology, and so forth. Although numerous how-to books on strategy formulation have also been published, I feel that there are not enough texts that systematically synthesize — not as individual parts — the truly meaningful essence of strategy, marketing and other related subjects in the business scene that require the pursuit of results while making actual decisions.

The theme of this book is learning how to strengthen the capability of envisioning appropriate directions or attractive strategic options by combining the environmental changes of the market and competitors with internal resources and capabilities of the company, and assuming the impact on your business. We refer to this capability as strategic thinking. The uniqueness of this book lies in its systematization, through use of a strategic management process and selected elements that form essential strategic judgment. With this in mind, this book contains 15 steps necessary to create attractive strategic options, which have been compiled into systematic steps. I have put together a systematic flowchart of the 15 steps essential for creating attractive strategic options just before the beginning of chapter 1.

This book is suitable for managers or business professionals who need to develop business strategies or who wish to improve their strategy development process within an organization. It is also designed for use in business school courses that focus on marketing and strategy-related issues, such as strategic management, strategic marketing, entrepreneurship, etc.

I hope this book becomes the backbone for the actions and decisions of professionals who are practicing strategy or marketing in the business world. Furthermore, nothing would make me happier than if I am able to contribute in some way towards building a stronger economy as the sum total of creating attractive products as well as solutions, and developing competitive businesses and winning companies through this work.

Eiichi "Eric" Kasahara
May 2015

Contents

The Flow and Elements of Strategic Management

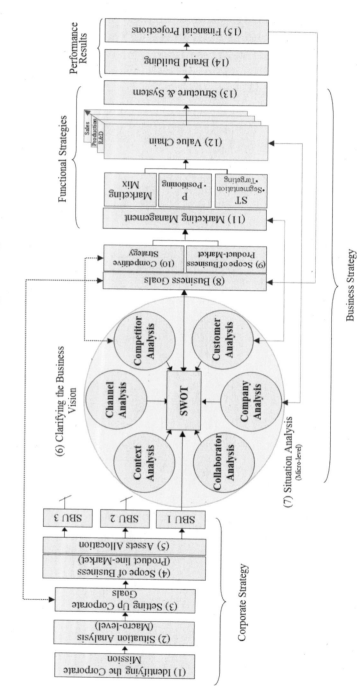

Chapter

1 The Essence of Strategic Management

In chapter 1, we will cover some important issues as the essence of strategic management. The issues are elements of strategic management, causes of disconnect between strategy and performance, strategic management as a scenario for success, flow and elements of strategic management, and contingency approach.

1.1 Elements of Strategic Management

We will begin by discussing why strategic management, which is defined as a system designed to help management make strategic decisions and create strategic vision, is largely considered dysfunctional. What is the reason behind the phrase, "strategic management is not functioning well"? Behind such statements, I think there is a case of, "although we started the business by giving considerable thought and created a strategy beforehand, we are not performing at the level that we expected to." Let's start by looking at the mechanism that determines performance.

The performance of a company is determined by its external factors (macro-economic environment or context, market or collection of customers and competition among competitors), internal factors (company resources), as well as the "action" that it takes. This can be simplified as follows:

$$\text{Performance} = f \text{ (external elements, internal elements, action)}$$

Strategic management functions as a guideline for specific actions to take in business situations within the mental model, as seen in Figure 1.1.

1

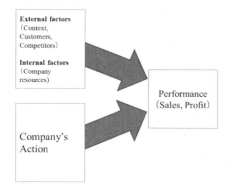

Source: Adapted from Saloner *et al*. (2001).

Figure 1.1.   Mental model concerning performance achievement.

Next, let's consider the structure of strategic management. So far, various strategic models have been proposed on the theory of strategic management. A classic framework would be Chandler's definition, which is: A strategy is to decide on a basic long-term goal, and to adopt the course for the action required to achieve that goal, and to allocate the required resources. Furthermore, there is the relatively recent Mintzberg's Emergent Strategy Model, which states that a strategy "needs to be systematically formulated beforehand, but also needs to be emergently created at the same time." Here, if we were to share strategic management at the minimum level that is required on a practical basis, I believe it could be sufficiently explained by referring to the following three points: present location (current situation), destination (goal), and the ways to get there. The ways to get there are usually expressed as the scope of business. In addition, clarifying the scope of business also helps to identify the company's competitors. Subsequently, the focus becomes how to create competitive advantages against those competitors.

Military strategy and strategic management are essentially the same thing. However, if I were to point out a difference between the two, military strategy attempts to directly attack the enemy by employing various tactics, as opposed to strategic management in which it is not possible to physically attack competitors. In other words, competition is played out by appealing to customers regarding your company's solutions. The deciding factors involve creating an edge through products or service quality, price competition, the ease of buying (accessibility), and convincing communication methods.

Strategy components are comprised of setting goals that fit with the external and internal factors, deciding on the scope of business in order to achieve those goals, as well as creating competitive advantages within that scope of business and finally, the scenario that actualizes the fulfillment of goals by combining these elements. What I mean by scope of business pertains to product lines or products for particular markets or groups of customers, and defining the scope of functions (vertical integration) that your own company will undertake.

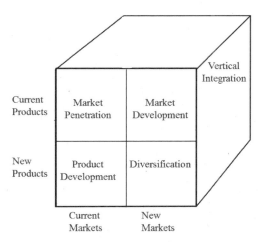

Figure 1.2.   Scope of business (product-market directions).

Source: Kasahara (2013).
Note: 4Cs = Company, Customers, Competitors and Context

Figure 1.3.   Components of strategic management.

1.2 Causes of Disconnect between Strategy and Performance

If the reason for the dysfunction of strategic management is due to performance not meeting expectations and the inability to achieve the set goals, then you must check the present situation analysis that was conducted. In other words, you will need to verify if there has been a thorough analysis of the external factors (macroscopic environment, market and competition) and internal factors (company resources). I often see cases where there is a significant amount of depth when it comes to company (resources) analysis and a certain degree of completion for the macroscopic environment analysis, but with a rather perfunctory market analysis. However, as for competitor analysis, the level of scrutiny appears as if the report was simply copied from some handy business journals. I recommend taking another look at your level of perception or awareness if you think that merely copying a report from a journal means the completion of an analysis. For competitor analysis, you need to get a grasp of your competitors. Unless you are able to understand the unmet needs of customers and future directions of competitors, it is very difficult to achieve success.

If the present situation analysis (external factors/environment and internal factors/resources) is sufficient, then the next checkpoint would be the compatibility between the present situation analysis and goals. By crosschecking the environment and resources, you should know if the goals set were in sync with the present state, or if they were adequately clarified. You need to set goals based upon SMART (Specific, Measurable, Achievable, Result-oriented, Time-bound) concept. This means that you must clearly specify an achievable level for your goals. Furthermore, it is important to fix these goals with a result-oriented and measurable index, and by being mindful of time.

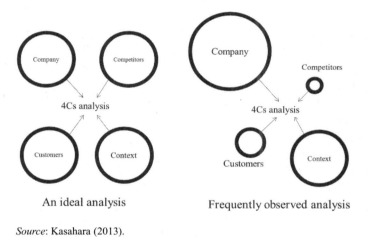

An ideal analysis   Frequently observed analysis

Source: Kasahara (2013).

Figure 1.4.   Ideal analysis vs. frequently observed analysis.

The next checkpoint is the compatibility between the goals and the scope of business. This refers to whether you have selected a scope of business that is appropriate for the goal. Regardless of how large the goal is or how mature the conventional scope of business is, continually spending your entire time on penetrating the market within that scope of business will clearly lead to a harsh result, no matter what tactics are employed. In that case, you must consider expanding the scope of business.

The next step is to verify if the selected scope of business has actualized, and maintained a relative advantage against existing as well as potential competitors. Put simply, competitive advantage refers to whether your business is able to provide products and services that customers believe have a higher value compared with those of your competitors. Similarly, it means whether there is a value chain that can provide products with the same benefit level at a lower cost than competitors.

1.3 Strategic Management is a Scenario for Success

Finally, you need to know whether a scenario exists that makes it possible to achieve the goals by combining the elements of strategic management. Have you ever received an opinion from executive managers after submitting a business plan or business strategy in the company you belong to, such as: "Overall it's not bad, and I don't really know what it is, but something is missing," or "Your strategy proposal lacks punch"? Let's look at the following message:

> Our strategy is to become the global leader in the market for mid-grade microwave ovens through mass production.

Is it clear whether the strategic elements are accurately included in the short message? The scope of business is the global market for mid-grade microwave ovens. Needless to say, the goal is to assume the position of global leader within that market. The competitive edge is low production cost or cost leadership. Although this proposition is somewhat simple and clear, I cannot see the scenario of how the company will specifically combine the elements that compose the strategy to achieve the No.1 global market share. For that reason, it falls short of delivering a message with punch. How about the next message?

> Quite a few finished-goods suppliers, such as companies manufacturing electronic home appliances in Japan and Europe, have been trying to increase their

efficiency by outsourcing production. In that process, we expect that the plants or manufacturing departments of those suppliers will become unnecessary. Our strategy is to purchase used production facilities from these manufacturers and expand our capacity, so as to enjoy what is called economies of scale. Subsequently, while utilizing those facilities, our plan is to substantially increase our production share as a contract manufacturer (the so-called EMS). From now on, we will secure fixed orders from the finished-goods manufacturers (= OEM) as the receiving end of their outsourcing. At the same time, we will continue to provide our own branded products with high cost performance for the market segment geared to the middle-and-lower class, without directly competing with the OEMs. This segment is expected to grow worldwide, and is quite attractive both in terms of volume and growth rate. We will contribute towards the growth of this segment while also expanding our share within this area. Our cost reduction plan is as follows:

(1) A product concept that specializes in basic functionality (cost reduction through design simplification);
(2) Hiring senior and skilled labour from finished-goods manufacturing companies (experience curve effect);
(3) Using open-modular type design (reducing production cost).

Finally, we will actualize an overwhelming competitiveness against our competitors by adopting a disruptive, low-cost strategy based on the aforementioned steps. At the same time, we will expand our share through world-wide e-commerce. Ultimately, we will apply this model to other home electronics besides microwave ovens, and will aim for a full line-up.

This message has a higher degree of completion in two ways. To begin with, it shows the strengthening of cost competitiveness through mass production and volume sales. Subsequently, it clearly lays out the scenario for increasing share within the target segment. The scenario also clarifies, through the company's resources and capabilities, the fundamental question as to why this is possible. Next, regarding the attractiveness of the target market segment, not only does it state that high growth is expected, but the message also logically explains the formation of a market that is sufficiently capable of absorbing a cost leadership strategy. For the rest, it should be enough to explain the preceding by using numbers during market analysis. If the assortment or combination of strategic components is what we call strategic planning, then strategic management includes a scenario or a story explaining how strategic elements such as goals, scope of business, and competitive advantage play out; how it facilitates fulfilling those goals; and how companies and businesses are led to succeed.

As stated by D'aveni and Gunther (1994), it is assumed that the period an average firm can sustain its competitiveness based upon a certain business model is

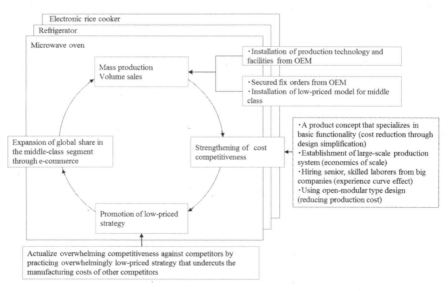

Source: Kasahara (2013).

Figure 1.5.   Strategic scenario/story.

becoming increasingly shorter these days. A firm may look as if it maintains competitive advantages based upon a certain robust business model. However, in reality, a firm that remains competitive renovates/reforms its business model quite often, resulting in sustained competitiveness. That is why I consider creating a scenario/story to achieve future visions and goals is paramount in strategic management.

As a summary of this chapter, I will list some basic differences between strategic planning and strategic management. As Aaker (2005, 2013) mentioned in one of his text books, the process of developing and implementing strategies has been described over the years using various terms such as budgeting, strategic planning and strategic management. All these terms have similar meanings; however, we need to be aware of vague but important distinctions existing between strategic planning and strategic management. The difference between the two is related to how you see the environment. If you think you are in a business with a lot of radical changes and unpredictable discontinuity, you need to be more responsive and proactive to customers and competitors and think and act on a real time basis outside the planning periodic cycle. Under such conditions, strategic management would

	Strategic Planning	Strategic Management
Assumptions	Incremental changes Predictable discontinuity	Radical changes Unpredictable discontinuity
Style	Environment is to be accepted Reactive & adaptive	Environment is to be influenced Proactive & interactive
Process	Periodic cycle	Real time
Tools	Analysis and planning	Assume and respond
Competition	Sustainable competitive advantages	Chain of temporary competitive advantages
Output	Strategic options that constitute a business model	Scenario/story to achieve strategic goals
In Charge	Management	Leaders and Staff

Figure 1.6. Differences between Strategic Planning and Strategic Management.

be the appropriate approach to take. Some of the basic differences between strategic planning and strategic management are enumerated in Figure 1.6.

1.4 Flow and Elements of Strategic Management

Many people hear the word "strategic management" and think of creating a business model that increases profitability in a particular business, or establishing specific ways to compete in a certain industry. If your company is a manufacturer consisting of a single business or relatively small company, then strategic management is indeed about building a strategy for one particular business. However, if you are a multi-business company, you should first consider how to allocate corporate assets or capital, such as human capital or manpower and financial capital or money before you set a specific strategy for each business unit. For this, you need to consider which scope of business to pursue in order to achieve sustainable growth for your company. A corporate strategy is for selecting growth areas for the overall company and setting asset allocation between those growth areas, while a business strategy aims to improve the competitive advantages and profitability of a particular business within the company. Simply put, a corporate strategy is concerned with the allocation of corporate assets, and business strategy focuses on the application of corporate assets. Let's look at the fundamental relationship between these two strategies.

A corporate strategy addresses mainly two questions: what businesses the corporation should be in and how the corporate office should allocate resources among these businesses. Kotler (2000) argued that a business should be viewed as a customer-satisfying process, not a goods-producing process in his book. Products could last or remain in place for a short time, but customer groups, their needs and solutions to their needs could last forever. I encouraged companies to redefine their businesses in terms of two elements. One of them is customer groups

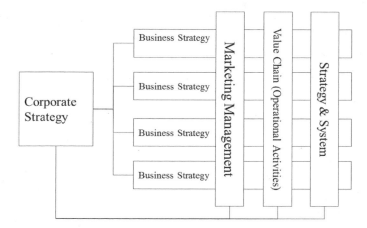

Figure 1.7. Major sub-systems of Strategic Management as a system.

Figure 1.8. Major components of a business strategy.

and the other one is solutions. For example, a high tech startup with disruptive lighting technologies defines its business as supporting theaters by proving highly advanced and dependable lighting systems. It can also expand into other businesses. For example, it can serve large sized retail chains by offering highly customized lighting systems with design service options.

A very small company may have only one business, but companies normally tend to manage different businesses. A strategic business unit (SBU) is a single business or collection of businesses that has its own competitors and customers and requires a distinctive strategy. Business strategy centers on how a company competes against competitors in a certain industry and positions itself among them. The focus of competitions is not among companies; rather, it is among their individual business units.

A business strategy includes a limited number of components, such as defining the scope of business supported by competitive strategy, marketing management, and a value chain that integrates operational activities. Those components can be viewed as the building blocks of a business strategy. In other words, a business strategy can be perceived as a set of integrated strategic components. A competitive strategy aims to clarify how the SBU can establish and sustain a long-term competitive position among its competitors in its chosen product-market scope.

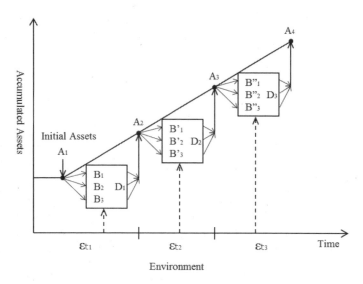

Source: Shimaguchi (2000).

Note: D = Domain or Scope of Business, B = Business.

Figure 1.9.   Corporate growth model.

Marketing management is for developing appropriate products/solutions for target customers within that scope. The value chain focuses on how resources allocated to the various operational areas can be used most efficiently and effectively to support the business strategies. In summary, corporate growth is the process of further enriching the company's accumulated assets by appropriately allocating and applying them to the relevant businesses, based on the business environment and corporate mission.

Strategy formation can be divided into the following steps:

(1) Identify the company's mission
(2) Analyze its macro-level situation (customers, competitors, company, and context)
(3) Set up corporate goals based upon its situation
(4) Define its scope of business (what products to which markets for achieving the above goals)
(5) Allocate assets among strategic business units / SBUs (product-market investment plan)
(6) Clarify the vision of each SBU
(7) Analyze its micro-level situation (customers, competitors, company, and context)
(8) Set up the SBU's goals based upon its SWOT (strengths, weaknesses, opportunities, and threats)
(9) Define the scope of business (what products to which markets for achieving the above goals)
(10) Develop competitive advantages among competitors in the scope (competitive strategy)
(11) Create value by providing solutions to target customers in the scope (marketing management)
(12) Develop a value chain that integrates all the operational activities to support the value proposition
(13) Build the infrastructure required to promote all the above actions (structure and system)
(14) Try to create the right brand identity (brand building)
(15) Develop a profit model (financial projections)

1.5 Contingency Approach in Strategic Management

As we see in the comparison between strategic planning and strategic management, it is believed that how to develop and execute strategies should be different, depending on the environmental predictability and the environmental interactivity of the business you are in. Environmental predictability refers to what extent changes in the market, competition, and the macro-economic climate can be predicted; meanwhile, environmental interactivity refers to the degree that a impact on the market and competition can be created proactively and independently by your firm.

Although the predictability of the industries in the top right quadrant of Figure 1.10 is low, environmental inter-activity is high. ICT and advanced medical equipment industries are examples in which there are many opportunities for changing the industry structure. As those industries have not yet been fully established and the barriers for entry are low, it is difficult to make assumptions on demand and competition. Strategic management may be the approach to be taken here.

In the top left quadrant, both environmental predictability and environmental interactivity are high. The airplane and defense industries are examples of this quadrant. Those are businesses that can achieve their future visions relatively independently.

A typical industry in the bottom left quadrant is the automobile industry, where environmental predictability is highly stable but interactivity is relative low. It is clear what will be the main issues for R&D in the automobile industry in the future. As you can imagine, safety or automatic driving systems and energy savings are the main issues for R&D, which every automobile manufacturer is highly aware of. However, even industry leaders such as Toyota or Volkswagen cannot fully control the industry structure. Numerous environmental elements, such as industry rules, government policies, and social values, should be considered when doing business. Strategic planning might be the appropriate approach to take.

Finally, the electronic device industry and building materials industry are examples of industries with both low environmental predictability and environmental interactivity.

Mintzberg (1998) pointed out that strategies consist of aspects in which the future is deliberately planned out, and strategy is emergently formed through the consideration, selection, and execution of strategic options considered as appropriate for the environmental changes. Strategies formed in an emergent manner are recognized as patterns when accompanying trends. Mintzberg also indicated that strategy has the aspect of perspective, or corporate vision, as well as clarifying the actual value provided to the market as the positioning of a given company's products on a positioning map, which expresses the value provided to the market on X and Y axes. While strategy is deliberately planned in advance and is concurrently formed in an emergent manner, the characteristics

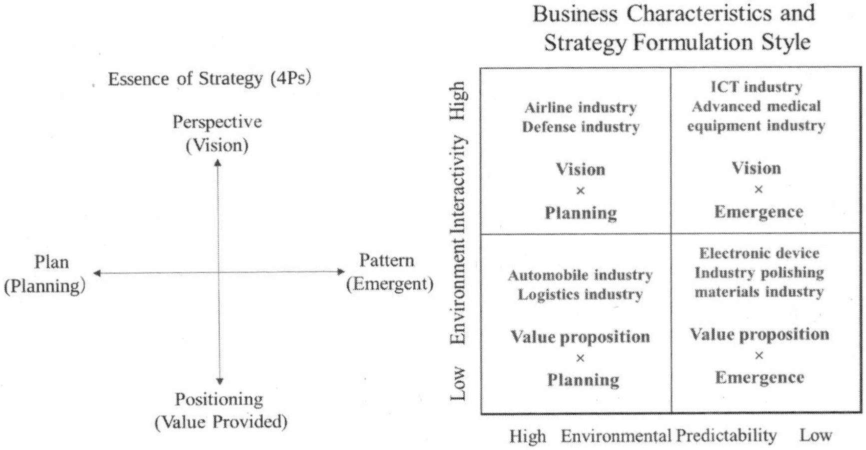

Source: Kasahara (2013).

Figure 1.10.   Contingent approach in strategic management.

of your business will determine whether to focus on deliberateness or emergence and what kind of approach should be taken in the strategy formulation process. It is believed that style in strategic management is contingent on the business environment.

Issues relating to strategic management, such as the level of flexibility required in executing strategies, the review period for strategies, selection of customers as strategic targets, relationships with targeted customers, and so on, should be considered based upon the nature of your business.

2 15 Steps of Strategic Management for Creating Attractive Strategic Options

As I have mentioned previously, the theme of this book is to share tips on how to strengthen the capability of envisioning appropriate directions and attractive strategic options (we refer to this capability as "strategic thinking"), while combining the environmental changes of the market and competitors with management resources and capabilities of the company, and immediately being able to surmise the impact on your business. I have selected 15 points that are regarded as being indispensable for creating attractive strategic options, and compiled them into systematic steps. The 15 steps are largely divided into three parts, and are analyzed under the subjects of "corporate strategy," "business strategy," and "performance results."

The following five subjects will be discussed under corporate strategy: (1) Identifying the corporate mission; (2) Macro-level situation analysis; (3) Setting up corporate goals; (4) Selecting the scope of business (product-market); and (5) Asset allocation (Product Portfolio Management/PPM). The following eight subjects will be covered under the theme of business strategy: (1) Clarifying the business vision; (2) Micro-level situation analysis; (3) Setting up business goals; (4) Defining the scope of business (product-market); (5) Competitive strategy; (6) Marketing management; (7) Designing the value chain/Synchronizing functional strategies with marketing; and (8) Developing the structure and systems.

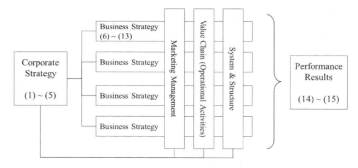

Figure 2.1.   15 steps that compose strategic management as a system.

Finally, performance results are monitored by: (1) Brand building and (2) Financial projections.

2.1 Corporate Strategy

A corporate strategy concerns mainly two questions: what businesses should the corporation be in, and how should the corporate office allocate assets among the strategic business units (SBUs).

2.1.1 *Corporate Mission*

A corporate mission defines the value that the company offers to society and the social role it should continue to fulfill. Why is it necessary to begin forming corporate strategy by identifying the corporate mission? It is because if your company's values are not clarified, subsequent choices concerning elements in the management strategy will become jumbled and unclear. Take, for instance, strategic analysis: if the mission is unclear, the boundaries of what to analyze become extremely ambiguous. The following is a list of messages that summarize the "values" of some relatively well-known companies.

"Dedication to every client's success" (IBM)
"Innovative and Practical Solutions" (3M)

"Inspire the Next" (Hitachi)
"make.believe" (Sony)
"Strive through 'C&C' to help advance societies
worldwide" (NEC)
"Emotional Engineering" (BMW)
"The Power of Dreams" (Honda)

Sharing an industry does not automatically create competition. Sony's "make.believe," for example, evidently embodies "the wish to create excitement in which people can become engrossed." Hitachi's message is "Inspire the Next," which can be interpreted as an intention to "encourage innovation in the next generation's social infrastructure." NEC intends to "achieve a user-friendly and eco-friendly information society through C&C innovation," and its scope of business is ICT ('C&C' stands for computers and communications). Although these three companies are positioned in the technology industry, the directions they are aiming for are quite different. This means their targets for competitor analysis also vary. Sony creates excitement that people can lose themselves in; so benchmarking targets will certainly include game console manufacturers such as Nintendo and Microsoft's Xbox. On the other hand, Hitachi's message is "Inspire the Next" — so perhaps companies that develop cutting-edge technologies are targeted in their competitor analysis. NEC, which competes in the arena of information society, may target IBM for competitor analysis, regardless of the establishment of a strategy for direct competition. Whether or not you establish a strategy of direct competition with the companies that you benchmark is a completely different matter. The point is that if you try to perform strategic analysis without a clear idea of your company's values, you won't be able to establish which customers, markets, competitors or industries to analyze, and inevitably your analysis will be ambiguous.

2.1.2 *Macro-level Situation Analysis*

As already mentioned, the main outputs of a corporate strategy are the definition of the scope of business or clarification of SBUs that are the units of strategy formation, and the appropriate allocation of assets among the units. Corporate strategy formulation calls for strategic analysis, which is to examine the potential growth of customers and markets, the company's relative advantages in comparison with its competitors, and the macro-environment that influences market growth.

The analysis shares the framework of the 4C analysis — customers and market (Customers), competitors and industry (Competitors), corporate assets (Company), and the macro-environment (Context) — which is also required in business strategy formulation. However, with business strategy it is necessary to consider how to preserve and increase competitive advantages over specific competitors and provide solutions to customers and markets. The level of analysis must be more specific in the process of business strategy development. Incidentally, macro-environment analysis covers politics, economy, society/culture, technology, environment/ecology, and law/regulations, and is generally known by its acronym PESTEL. These are understood to be the context, or the important elements that underlie society.

Macro-environment = context = PESTEL.

As for the flow of analysis, after completing the 4C analysis, you then separate them into four categories: S (Strengths) for elements that you can control and have a positive influence, W (Weaknesses) for elements that you can control and have a negative influence, O (Opportunities) for elements that you cannot control and have a positive influence, and T (Threats) for elements that you cannot control and have a negative influence. This is the so-called

SWOT analysis. For further details on the 4C analysis, please refer to the situation analysis framework explained in business strategy development.

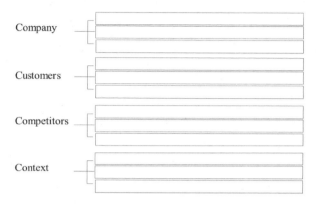

Figure 2.2. 4C analysis.

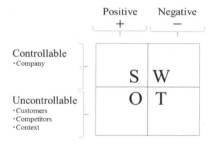

Figure 2.3. SWOT cross analysis.

2.1.3 *Corporate Goals*

The SWOT analysis enables the setting of corporate goals within the plan's period (on a realistic and specific level). Through it you are able to understand to an extent the scale and growth prospective of the market, as well as your relative competitive advantages over competitors. You can now establish corporate goals with reference to the corporate mission, and plan targets submitted by each unit. You should establish goals with measurable indicators, such as sales, profits, and market share, etc. The more specific the goal is, the more motivating it becomes. Of course, it must be a feasible goal, as an ideal degree of feasibility makes you think, "It won't be easy, but it's not impossible. I'll take on this challenge!" I believe this is where management is considered a combination of science and art.

How you establish elements in the corporate strategy, including goals, will differ greatly depending on the circumstances; for example, if changes are stable in the business environment, making future predictions is relatively straightforward, and the company's active efforts can quite easily change the market, competition, systems, and laws. Conversely, if there are intense changes in the business environment, then making predictions becomes difficult and the company's efforts will have little impact on the market and competition. When future predictions are simple and there is a high degree of environmental interaction, then the goals act as guidelines for practicing management that should be observed, and also provide a basis for regulation. However, when future predictions are difficult and there is a low degree of environmental interaction, I believe that the goals should be regarded as a reference for testing hypotheses through trial and error.

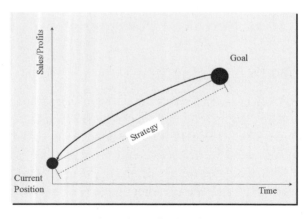

Figure 2.4.   Goal setting.

Flexibly adapting to environmental changes should be prioritized over compliance, and the goals should be considered as a springboard from which initial ideas are corrected in order to improve the strategy.

2.1.4 *Scope of Business*

Once your goals are clear, you can then establish the scope of business that is the arena in which to accomplish those goals. The scope of business can be defined by two axes: what customers or market you will target, and what products or solutions you will offer. In general, this is expressed with a product-market growth matrix. Normally, the current scope of business is expressed with the market (collection of customers) on the horizontal (X) axis and the product (solution) on the vertical (Y) axis. Each cell is a business unit (BU). Each BU or set of integrated BUs that provides the basis of strategy formation is called a strategic business unit (SBU).

		Market			
		I	II	III	IV
Product	A	Business A			
	B		Business B		
	C		Business C		
	D				

Figure 2.5.   Scope of business (Product Lines-Market).

Figure 2.5 shows three SBUs: A, B, and C. To examine the potential of each unit, you need to evaluate the market size, market growth rate, and the company's market share for each BU (the smallest business unit composed of each product and market) within the SBU. The market size is represented by the size of the circle, the market growth rate by an arrow, and the company's share by a pie block in the circle.

Consider the scope of business expressed in Figure 2.6 below. Although the company seems to be sufficiently large, significant market growth cannot be expected in this scope of business.

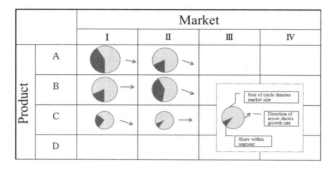

Figure 2.6. Current situation.

However, let's say you want to promote a strategy for increasing share with the current products and markets (this is called market penetration strategy). What measures can you take? It will be necessary to steal customers from competitors, increase the frequency of use of your product by existing customers, increase the amount of your product used each time, or find customers who have never used your product from the existing markets.

On the other hand, employing a strategy to aim for growth by releasing an existing product into a new market is called market development. An example of this is to release an existing product into emerging markets in Asia, South America, Russia, or Africa, which are expected to grow in the future. It includes expanding not only to geographically new markets, but also expanding the target market to, for example, small- to mid-sized companies, micro-companies, or households.

In contrast, employing a strategy to aim for growth by releasing a new product into the current market is called product development. In addition to tangible products, the development of intangible products, such as designs, services, and consulting, is also considered product development.

The last direction is diversification, which is to enter into a new market, creating a new product for that market. Diversification does not guarantee that you will immediately do well in the new market, and naturally, the more appealing a market is the fiercer the competition will be. As there is a great deal of uncertainty, diversification is the direction with the most risk.

Companies proceed with market penetration while also considering other business possibilities for growth, such as market development, product development, or diversification. Each business has different roles, returns, and risks; so the allocation of assets, such as manpower and capital, will also differ. The next issue is how to allocate limited management assets among multiple business units.

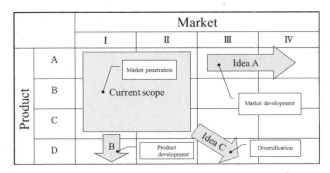

Figure 2.7.   Future directions.

Let's look at what will happen if we consider the possibilities of foreign markets using the product-market growth matrix on the previous page. It is not reasonable to consider the possibilities of targeting all global markets from the very beginning. I would recommend doing a double screening when considering global expansion. First, select indicators that have a high correlation with the diffusion rate of the product or solution you wish to offer, and use the indicators to select 5–10 regional markets that seem attractive. Then, use specific evaluation indicators to narrow down your target regions. Consider the following indicators that are generally used to assess foreign markets.

(1) Level of economic growth
(2) Population growth rate
(3) Economic infrastructure
(4) Cultural similarities
(5) Geographical proximity
(6) Political risks

Although these indicators are not completely off target, I believe they are not exactly precise. Let's look at one case study.

Nestlé's Global Expansion

When Nestle was considering global expansion for its instant coffee business, it established several groups to promote global expansion based on coffee consumption

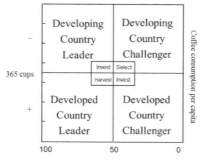

Source: Kotabe and Helsen (2010).
Note: Quadrants with low shares of coffee powder comprise mainly R&G coffee (roast and ground coffee).

Figure 2.8.   Nestlé's case.

per capita and share of instant coffee-for-home out of total coffee consumption. I am sure these indicators allowed for a remarkably more accurate evaluation of the marketability of the business in question than an economic index such as GDP per capita.

How to Select Evaluation Indicators

Now, let's say you are a manufacturer of dishwashers. When considering global expansion, what indicators do you think you should use for the first screening? Our research shows that compared to GDP or population growth rates, variables such as the employment rate of women and household size are more persuasive toward

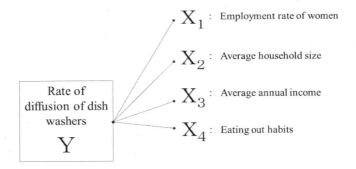

Figure 2.9.   Use of indicators to evaluate marketability.

External (market) attractiveness	Importance (1-5)	Region -A-	Region -B-	Region -C-	Region -D-
Market size					
Market growth rate					
Competition					
Market profitability					
Internal (resource) fitness	Importance (1-5)	Region -A-	Region -B-	Region -C-	Region -D-
Technology/R&D fitness					
Production/facilities fitness					
Sales force/channel fitness					
Share/competitive position					
Total					

Evaluation: 5 highly positive, 1 highly negative
Importance: 5 very important, 1 least important

Figure 2.10.   Comparison of markets of foreign regions.

the targeted variable, the diffusion rate of dishwashers. You should use these types of indicators in your global expansion efforts in order to effectively narrow down the target to a highly potential foreign market. For your reference, Figure 2.10 shows examples of indicators for a somewhat specific second screening, to be used on the regions selected in the first screening.

2.1.5 *Allocation of Assets and Resources*

The final stage in the formulation of corporate strategy is the allocation of assets. You have already established your company's scope of business with the product-market growth matrix. So the next step is asset allocation, which is to determine how much of your limited and valuable assets and resources, which are basically human capital (people) and financial capital (money), should be allocated to each business (SBU) in the clarified scope of business. Put more eloquently, you must decide on the appropriate level of investment in each SBU. That is, you need to determine which SBUs to supply fewer assets to and which SBUs to supply more assets to. A tool used during this stage is Product Portfolio Management (PPM), which involves managing combinations of your products. Although the word product is used, the general rule is to consider the unit to be each SBU that is an independent business. PPM would be meaningless unless each unit were a profit center that pursues profit with responsibility over its particular assets. The point here is how to allocate assets; so if, say, a sales person is in charge of multiple products, this means the products share the sales person who is a management asset. In this case, it would not make sense to allocate assets by product. Asset allocation should be conducted among SBUs.

As mentioned above, Product Portfolio Management (PPM) is a tool used for asset allocation. One well-known example is the matrix developed by the Boston Consulting Group (BCG). Each SBU is plotted onto a matrix with the vertical (Y) axis expressing market growth rate and the horizontal (X) axis expressing relative share (your company's share divided by the share of the top share competitor) on logarithmic.

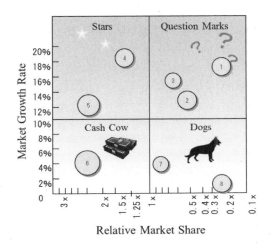

Figure 2.11.   The BCG's growth-share matrix (quantitative evaluation).

The SBUs can be categorized into four groups:

(1) Problem children/Question marks

Problem children (also known as question marks) are business units operating in rapidly growing markets, but having low market shares. In most cases, they are starting points for new businesses. Question marks have possibility to gain market share and become stars, and finally cash cows when markets get matured. If they fail to be market leaders, they will be regarded as dogs on declining stages. Question marks are SBUs that require capital investment in order to increase their relative shares.

(2) Stars

Stars are business units that make money because of their large market shares, but require investments for competition due to rapidly growing markets. They are graduated question marks. When market growth slows, if they remain as market leaders, they become cash cows. Otherwise they become dogs due to their low relative market share.

(3) Cash cows

Cash cows are SBUs that provide stable cash flow because of their large market shares in slow-growing or mature markets. These units typically generate cash in excess of the amount of cash needed to maintain the businesses. They are expected to be the funding base for question marks and stars.

(4) Dogs

Dogs are SBUs in mature markets that are not able to obtain market shares. They are units with low market shares in mature markets. From an accounting point of view, such units are worthless, not generating enough cash for the company. They tend to deteriorate corporate value because of their low return on investment or assets. They are theoretically to be sold out.

This portfolio model supports decision-making for investment, so that revenue generated by cash cows and capital gained by reorganizing dogs are to be invested in the problem children/question marks, in order to develop them into stars or cash cows.

Business portfolios include various models, such as the quantitative BCG model, qualitative model, and a model that expresses the evolutionary life cycle (four stages of development, growth, decline, and maturity) on the vertical axis.

In all models, the vertical axis represents market attractiveness. Specifically, an SBU plotted in the upper quadrant is generally attractive, and therefore it is competitive and requires investment. On the other hand, an SBU plotted in the lower quadrant is less attractive and therefore it is not as competitive, so investment should be restrained

Ability to Compete

	High	Medium	Low
Low	1	1	2
Medium	1	2	3
High	2	3	3

Market Attractiveness

1. Invest/grow
2. Selective investment
3. Harvest/divest

Evaluating the Ability to Compete
- Technology skills
- Patents
- Flexibility
- Distribution
- Marketing
- Organization
- Share by segment
- Customer loyalty
- Margins
- Growth

Evaluating Market Attractiveness
- Size
- Growth
- Competition: quantity, types, effectiveness, commitment
- Price levels
- Profitability
- Technology
- Governmental regulations
- Customer satisfaction levels
- Sensitivity to economic trends

Source: Adapted from Aaker (2005).

Figure 2.12.   Market attractiveness-competitive-position portfolio (qualitative evaluation).

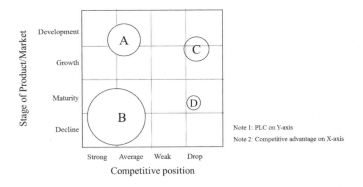

Source: Adapted from Hofer and Schendel (1978).

Figure 2.13.   Product-market evolution portfolio matrix.

and directed to another SBU. Regarding the vertical axis, an SBU positioned on the left hand has a competitive advantage and holds a higher share, and therefore produces higher returns and requires less investments due to economies of scale and the experience curve effect. An SBU on the right hand has less competitive advantages and a lower share, and therefore produces lower returns and requires more investments because it cannot benefit from economies of scale and the experience curve effect. So you can see here how a company can clarify the positions and roles of its business with just two axes.

As for techniques when creating your matrix, first note how you identify your relative share. If your company holds a top market share, relative market share is derived by dividing your market share by the market share of the second top company. If your company holds

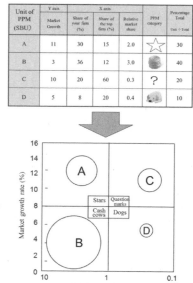

*Relative share:

The share of your company ÷ the share of the top company.

The share of your company ÷ the share of the second largest company (when your company has the top share)

Note: The mid-point on the Y-axis should represent the average growth rate of markets, or the average cost of financing as a company (weighted average cost of capital=WACC).

Figure 2.14.   Worksheet for PPM.

second or lower market share, it is derived by dividing your market share by the market share of the top company. The relative market share axis should be measured using a ratio scale. The mid-point is 1, the left edge is 10, and the right edge is 0.1. Finally, the size of the circles should represent the current business scale of each business (sales). I recommend using the worksheet in Figure 2.14 when actually creating your matrix.

Criticism of the PPM

The following are some criticisms of the PPM:

- It is too simple to be realistic. (Market attractiveness is not only about growth rate, and competitive advantage is not only about market share.)
- The method ignores the development of new businesses.
- The interrelation between businesses is overlooked.
- The names of each quadrant may cause misunderstandings.
- It takes time to include it into the process of businesses management.
- It will result in an over-concentration of human resources and power in the management planning division.
- PLC is not always accurate, and a company's efforts may cause a market to grow.
- Cost reduction does not only depend on the experience curve effect, but is also possible through open innovation.
- The method does not consider the synergy between business units.

Some of the above come close to being false accusations. The point is that you should consider the fundamental matter of asset allocation (that is, what level of return can you expect from each SBU) and use the method effectively. I hope, at least, that you will not give out a message that your company should defend each and every business to the very last, and attack, attack, attack! If you must make a declaration, make it this: Clarify where to attack, defend, cut, and abandon!

2.2 Business Strategy

Now, we can finally start to consider business strategy, the most "strategy-like" type of its kind. In section 2.1, we used PPM to undertake a corporate-centric examination of the allocation of resources among the multiple businesses that make up a corporation. With business strategy, the specific business units that are shown in the PPM circles take center stage. Business strategy centers on how a firm competes in a given industry and positions itself among its competitors. The focus of competition is not among companies, but among business units that should be planned separately from the rest of the company. The core unit for developing a business strategy is called an SBU, which has the following characteristics:

It is a single business or collection of related businesses that should be planned separately from the other businesses in the company.

- It is made up of products and markets.
- It has its own strategy and leader.
- It has its own competitors and customers.
- It functions as a profit center, seeking to make a profit.
- It is able to exercise discretionary control over certain resources.

When senior management allocates resources (people and money) to a business, the dominant role shifts from the senior management team to the head of the individual business unit. If we use PPM to show this, we should be thinking in terms of how the business unit manager utilizes the resources that have been allocated to them to both increase the size of the business unit's circle

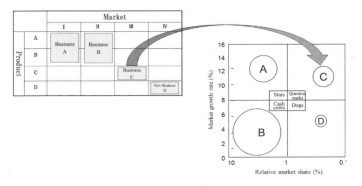

Figure 2.15. The unit of business strategy.

(i.e. boost sales) and achieve a leftward shift (i.e. grow the business unit's market share).

To this end, future goals are set on the basis of the present state and future prospects, and strategies are formulated in order to achieve these goals. That is to say, analysis is performed with respect to the current situation (including the future outlook) of the business unit, providing a basis for setting targets that are achievable by the business unit in question. The methods that will be adopted in order to achieve these targets are then selected. Methods here refer to what kind of products and services will be supplied to which markets; in other words, defining the scope of the business unit's activities and clarifying its competitive positioning.

Defining the scope of your business involves deciding on a given market and then identifying the competitors who are already doing business with your target customers, or who may start doing business with them in the future. This means that one of the key aspects of business strategy is clarifying your company's competitive positioning within the selected business areas. After comparing your competitors with your company, if it appears that your company has the advantage, then you may decide to go into direct competition with these competitors. If, on the other hand, it seems that you have little chance of defeating them, then you can adopt a strategy that avoids direct competition.

Whereas with corporate strategy, emphasis is placed on choosing a scope of business and concentrating resources where they can be used to best effect, with business strategy the main focus is on defining the selected scope of business in detail and clarifying the company's competitive advantages there. The essence of a business strategy is to create competitive advantages in the scope of business by proving unique values to the selected customers, supported by functional strategies and programs. Here we examine business strategy using the strategy steps outlined below: Clarifying the business vision, micro-level situation analysis, setting up business goals, defining the scope of business (product-market), competitive strategy, marketing management, designing the value chain/synchronizing operational activities with marketing, and developing the structure and systems.

The concept described in Figure 2.16 is something that we are supposed to have set up prior to developing a business strategy. The concept can be developed through

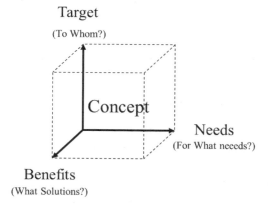

Figure 2.16   Concept.

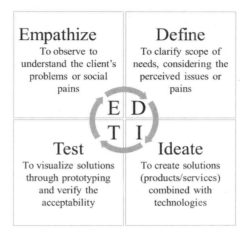

Empathize	Define
To observe to understand the client's problems or social pains	To clarify scope of needs, considering the perceived issues or pains
Test	**Ideate**
To visualize solutions through prototyping and verify the acceptability	To create solutions (products/services) combined with technologies

Note: Adapted from IDEO and Nonaka and Takeuchi (1995).

Figure 2.17.   EDIT.

the so-called EDIT process, which stands for empathize, define, ideate and test. 'Empathize' means to observe to understand the client's or market's issues or social pains. 'Define' means to clarify the scope of the needs, considering the perceived issues and pains. 'Ideate' is to create solutions combined with technologies, products, and services. 'Test' is to visualize solutions through prototypes and verify the acceptability.

Ideation or idea generation is based on customer inconvenience with the current situation. The following are the key elements for ideation.

- Problems/social pains in general
- Current situation resluted in by the current solutions
- Satisfaction level with the current situation
- Ideal situation
- Unmet needs or the gap between the ideal situation and the current situation
- Hypothetical solutions (products or services, functions, performance, specifications)
- Necessary technologies for supporing the solutions

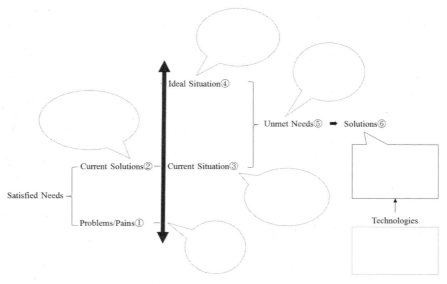

Figure 2.18   Needs structure.

2.2.1 *Business Vision*

With both business strategy and corporate strategy, it is a good idea to start by clarifying your values. "Without value, there is no strategy; without strategy, there is no effective sales activity; without sales activity, there are no orders; without orders, there is no life!" This was a remark by a senior manager at the sales division of a major corporation, which made a deep impression on me. When value is expressed in words, it can take the form of a mission or vision.

A mission can be regarded as a company's social role, in terms of what kind of value it provides for society as a whole. One might say that the mission is the path that a company believes it should take. The importance of a mission to a company goes without saying; it has been made abundantly clear by the ill-advised path taken by those banks that forgot their mission of providing support for the industry, and the horrendous negative impact that this had on the global economy. A major aspect of corporate strategy is the selection of an attractive scope of business based on the company's mission (i.e. the direction that the company feels it should be moving in), and then prioritizing its concentration of resources there.

Why is it that, when thinking in terms of business strategy, a company needs to focus on what it wants to achieve and what it wants to be? This is because, by keeping in mind the mission that outlines the company's overall direction and sharing a concrete picture of what the company wants to achieve and also what it wants to become, which reflects the environment in which the business unit in question has to operate, then the staff in charge of running the business unit can pool their energy to maximum effect.

The company's vision is a concrete expression of what the company wants to achieve and what it wants to be. Many companies have consistently held to a vision of defeating overseas competitors. By and large, those companies that have remained true to this vision have succeeded in surviving and growing, despite today's challenging business environment. By contrast, those companies that have lost competitiveness lack a sense of the importance of being able to come out on top in global competition.

A company's vision can be of one of the following types:

- Dream-driven
  Becoming a world leader in renewable energy; creating the world's fastest computer; going to Mars; saving people who suffer from terrible diseases, etc.
- Number-driven
  Growing the company's market share by 30%; achieving double-digit earnings growth; doubling annual sales revenue within three years, etc.

There are cases where these two types of vision are combined into one. Basically, this applies in the situation where a dream-driven type of vision is adopted, but then when the time comes to implement it, the vision is expressed in terms of numbers for the benefit of the staff who will actually be implementing it.

2.2.2 *Micro-level Situation Analysis: What is the Present State and Future of the Business?*

When carrying out a present state analysis of a business for the purpose of formulating a business strategy, the overall framework used — in terms of the items analyzed — is broadly similar to that used for corporate strategy. The fundamental element is 4C analysis, which is the analysis of Customers, Competitors, Company and Context. However, with business strategy, given the need to clarify your company's competitive positioning with respect to the selected business areas, the analysis needs to be performed on a more detailed level.

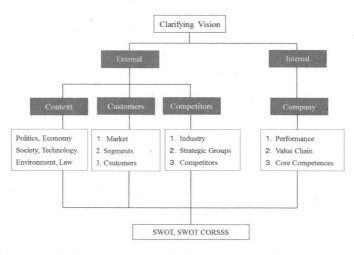

Figure 2.19. System diagram for business strategy formulation.

Customer analysis

When conducting customer analysis, it is recommended to use the following sequence: (1) Start off by identifying the market as a whole, seen as a collection of customers (buyers); (2) Perform an analysis of individual segments, i.e. groups of customers that have similar preferences; (3) Examine the needs of individual customers in the major segments. With this approach, you start off with a macro perspective that considers the market as a whole, and then move on to the micro perspective in relation to individual customers.

First, with regard to the market as a whole, secondary sources can be used to examine market size, market growth potential, market revenue potential, product life cycle, and so forth. The overall market analysis has two primary objectives: (1) to determine the attractiveness of the market and (2) to detect threats and opportunities in the market.

Next, we can proceed to divide the market into groups of similar preferences (i.e. segments), that would respond differently from other groups to your offering, and then make a segment-by-segment determination regarding attractiveness (in terms of segment size and segment growth potential) and the company's own competitiveness (based on segment-specific KBFs or key buying factors influencing purchasing decisions, the degree KBFs fit with the company's own products and services, and the company's market share in each segment). The necessary factors to consider when determining the basis for segmentation vary between the consumer goods market or business to consumer market and the industrial goods market or business to business market. The following list should help to clarify the differences:

- Classification criteria for the business to consumer market (examples):
  - Demographic variables: age, income, gender, occupation, social class
  - Behavioral variables: purpose, frequency of purchasing, purchasing experience, attitude
  - Geographic variables: country, region, metropolitan/suburban/rural
  - Psychographic variables: lifestyle, concerns, personality.

- Classification criteria for the business to business market (examples):
  - Variables relating to the purchasing company/organization: sector, form of organization, industry,

company size (large, SME, micro-companies), strategic positioning (leader company, follower company, or other), target market (high-end, low-end).

o Variables relating to purchasing conditions: purchasing status (new buy, re-buy, modified re-buy), purchasing experience, capabilities (level of service required)

o Variables relating to purchasing behavior: purchasing frequency/quantity (large, medium small), buying center (size, structure), purchasing criteria (technology, cost, after-sales service, etc.), purchasing/procurement style (centralized/unitary or dispersed).

The following are the basic steps for segmentation.

Step 1: To identify customer groups or segments.

Step 2: To clarify major key buying factors in each segment.

Step 3: To clarify segment attractiveness (external viewpoint) and strategic fit or competitive advantage (internal viewpoint) in each segment.

The final unit in customer analysis is the main individual customers in those segments, which are identified as being attractive by the segment analysis described above. While some companies implement regular customer

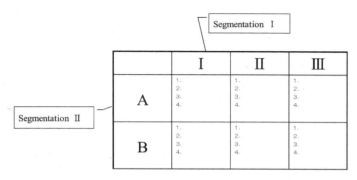

Note: Key buying factors (KBFs) are presented in order of importance.

Figure 2.20.   To identify customer groups or segments.

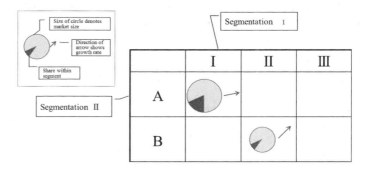

Figure 2.21.   Identifying the strategic segments that should be prioritized.

satisfaction surveys (at a frequency of at least once a year), other companies carry out field surveys in which the company's sales manager and chief technical officer work as a pair, visiting key clients to familiarize themselves with the key person at the client's buying center, and to directly find out what needs these key managers feel are not being met. The unmet needs of customers should be clarified through interviews, surveys, and observations. The following are some of the points to be identified for clarifying the unmet needs of customers:

- What elements of the product do customers value most?
- What are the customers' objectives?
- What are they really buying?
- Why are some customers dissatisfied?
- Why are some customers changing suppliers?
- What are the unmet needs that customers can identify?
- What is the incidence of customer problems?

Figure 2.22 summarizes the three steps used in customer analysis.

Competitor Analysis

When analyzing your competitors, it is recommended that you start by: (1) Analyzing the structure of the industry to which your company and your competitors all belong.

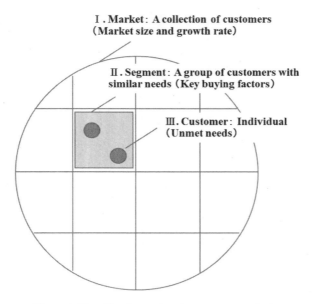

Figure 2.22.   The three steps in customer analysis.

An industry is a group of firms that offer a product or a class of products that are close substitutes for one another. The next step is: (2) Clarifying what strategic groups are forming within the industry. Finally: (3) Seeking to forecast likely developments in relation to the competitors within your strategic group or in relation to individual competitors that you need to watch closely.

The first step is to collate information regarding the following five aspects of industry structure: negotiating power of buyers, negotiating power of suppliers, threats from new entrants, threats from substitute products, and the nature of the competitive rivalry among those companies already active in the industry.

Buyers include corporations, institutions, individuals, households, and so on. The negotiating power of buyers is determined by the amount of choice available to them, and by how high the cost of switching to another supplier is. If there are a large number of vendors offering similar products or services, then the buyer's bargaining power will be strengthened. In an extreme case, with heavily commoditized products, price becomes the only meaningful source of differentiation.

Suppliers provide the modules, parts or raw materials needed to create a company's finished products. In the case of a limited number of suppliers, or when suppliers are able to exert oligopolistic control over an industry, then the bargaining power of suppliers will increase. The supplier's bargaining power will also increase if, from the buyer's perspective the cost of switching suppliers is high. When I worked as a consultant in the auditing sector, I was surprised at the amount of repeat business that auditing companies received despite frequently low levels of customer satisfaction. This was because the cost of switching to another auditor was too high for the client; every time a company switches to a different auditor, it has to let another group of people in on its business secrets.

The threat from new entrants relates to how high the barriers to entry are in the industry. In industries where participant companies require permits to operate, and in industries where the initial investment required to move into that business area is very high, the threat from new entrants will generally be low. On the other hand, if an industry experiences deregulation so that the direct barriers to entry are lowered, then there may be a sudden and dramatic fall in profit margins.

The greater the number of substitute products, the lower the profit margins will be in that industry. Substitute products are not competitor products, but rather products that eliminate the whole *raison d'être* of the existing products. Examples include Wii Fit in relation to conventional gyms, or wireless technology in relation to a car's wire harness.

The final stage of competitor analysis is to clarify the relationships among existing companies that are in direct competition with each other. During the growth stage of the PLC, even if new competitors enter the market, because the market as a whole is still expanding, the intensified competition is unlikely to have a serious negative impact on profitability. However, once the maturity stage is reached, the less dominant companies will seek to grow their market share using differentiation to challenge the top players, which in turn will force the market leaders to try and differentiate themselves; such a situation will place a downward pressure on profits.

The industry structure analysis model presented above is usually referred to as the "5 Forces Model", which is ideally suited for determining how profitable a given industry is likely to be.

We can now move on to competitor analysis. Here, a grid is used to categorize companies and determine the extent to which the competitors in the same industry are really in direct competition with one another. This form of analysis is referred to as strategic group analysis.

The dimensions used to classify competitors into strategic groups might include, for example, profit margin and market share. A large market share implies that a company has high sales and is able to benefit from economies of scale, while a high profit margin is likely to indicate that a company has successfully implemented some form of differentiation strategy. By determining what category your company falls into, you can then identify which competitors you need to watch carefully.

- Determine which strategic factors the X and Y axes denote (e.g. value added, profit margin, market share, sales volume, etc.)
- Decide the scale for the X and Y axes (determining the center-point)
- Collect data and create plots for individual companies
- Use the size of each circle to denote sales volume
- Examine the relative positioning of your company and other companies

The final step is to try to forecast the future trends relating to not only those competitors that are already part of the same strategic group as your company, but also those companies that you may compete with sometime in

PC Industry

【New Entrants】

No barrier exists

- An EMS factory can be set up for US$1 million
- Assembly technology (innovative technology is not required.)
- Many channels are available
- Low loyalty
- Low switching cost

【Suppliers】

Most PC value is created by suppliers

- OS by Microsoft
- CPU by Intel
- Monopolized by these two

【Rivalry】

Intense competition among competitors

- Difficult to differentiate by hardware
- Difficult to take leadership (IBM)
- Slow growth
- Imitable technology
- +Competition for more security

【Buyers】

More bargaining power
- Limited budget for PCs
- +Strong needs for security
- More knowledgeable customers
- Low brand loyalty
- Less need for services
- Perfect price information available through the Internet

【Substitutes】

Many substitutes

- Home TVs are becoming more like PCs
- Many substitutes such as tablets, smart phones, wearable PCs, etc

Notes:
- indicates a negative factor.
+ indicates a positive factor.

Figure 2.23.   Clarifying the industry structure.

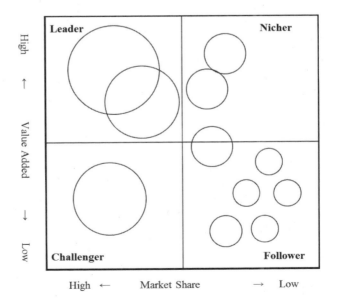

Note: The size of each circle indicates gross profit.

Figure 2.24.   Strategic group.

the future. When seeking to forecast future activity as part of competitor analysis, besides identifying the current positioning, you also need to pay attention to existing and latent competitors' strategic intentions.

More specifically, you need to compare the vision and goals of competitors with their current performance, and gauge whether or not they are likely to deem their current performance as satisfactory. If their performance falls below the level that they would consider satisfactory, then you need to consider if the competitor can achieve its performance targets by continuing with its current strategy, and if not, whether it will be possible for them to implement a new strategy successfully given their current operational resources and capabilities.

When considering future strategy, you need to take account of target markets, products, price, place, promotion, and personal selling. While you may be tempted to think that you can complete a competitor analysis just by citing some data from the competitor's financial statements, this is a very risky approach to take. Competitor analysis should involve the use of a wide range of data sources, including the data derived from customers, suppliers, and market research companies. You need to collate data from the competitor's website, investor relations (IR) materials, announcements made at conferences, securities reports, and other information sources, and then use your professional expertise and insight to try to get a sense of the competitor's strategic direction. The figures below summarize the various elements that constitute competitor analysis.

An overall schematic view of the industry and a competitor analysis is shown in Figures 2.25 and 2.26. Similarly, the former CEO of GE, Jack Welch used to ask his executives the following questions:

(1) Describe the global competitive environment where you operate
(2) In the last two years, what have your competitors done?

(3) In the same period, what have you done to them in the marketplace?

(4) How might they attack you in the future?

(5) What are your plans to leapfrog them?

Items \ Competitors			
Corporate Mission			
Goals/Objectives			
Assets/Functions (Characteristics)			
Planning			
R&D			
Production			
Sales			
Brand			
Current Performance			

Figure 2.25.   Present state of competitors.

Items \ Competitors			
Future Scope of Business			
Expected Marketing Strategy			
Target			
Product			
Price			
Place			
Promotion			
Expected Functional Strategies (R&D, Production, etc.)			

Figure 2.26.   Competitor strategy forecasting.

Company Analysis

When analyzing the resources available to your company, it is easier to clarify problems and develop hypotheses for

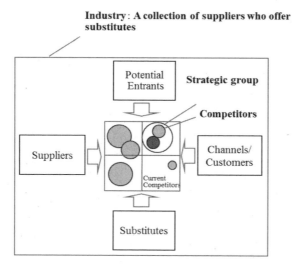

Figure 2.27. Competitor and industry analysis.

solving these problems if you start by reviewing the company's operational performance. Once you have developed a rough hypothesis, you can analyze the value chain and core competences to refine and also verify the hypothesis (as far as it is practicable).

When reviewing operational performance, it is advisable to make use of a line graph with time-series data for at least the past three years (and preferably five years), using the following indicators: sales, gross profit (value-added), operating profit, operating cash flow, cost ratio, gross margin ratio, operating profit ratio, sales per employee, gross profit per employee, operating profit per employee, customer concentration, sales per customer, quality level, new product development ratio (sales of new products divided by sales of all products), customer satisfaction, and so forth. If there are any unusual movements seen in the line graph, you should check the reason for them. Ideally, rather than just examining the indicators noted above at the company-wide level, they should also be broken down by customer segment, product, region, channel, and so on, with time-series data. This will make it easier to identify the areas where serious problems exist.

It goes without saying that an analysis of your company is intended to clarify its strengths and weaknesses. However, if the only data used for this analysis is related to your company, useful comparisons cannot be made. As far as possible, you should try to collect data for other companies that your company is in competition with, and then process this data so that it can be examined in parallel with your company's data. Once all the data has been properly collated, you should be able to carry out a performance comparison from three perspectives: between internal units, over time, and between your company and competitors. Looking at different aspects in this way will give you a clearer picture of the overall situation, and also make it easier to identify problems.

Having obtained a multi-faceted picture of your company's performance, you can now move on to the next step. Here, we seek to clarify the reasons for your company's strengths and weaknesses by integrating this examination with value-chain analysis. Value chain here refers to the conversion process from inputs to outputs, viewed in a time-series form. Clearly identifying the key activities in terms of R&D, marketing, engineering, manufacturing, sales, and so forth, will enable you to list the ways in which these factors help to boost performance. As for these factors — or performance drivers — you should endeavor to collect materials that relate not only to your own company, but also to your competitors. By treating the strengths and weaknesses of your company and competitors in relation to the value chain as explanatory variables (independent variables) and good or bad performance as the target variable (dependent variable), and by taking into account the possible causal relationships between the two, the real reasons behind a slump in performance can be identified, making it easier to develop a hypothesis as to how to achieve improvement.

Regarding the value chain, you should seek to determine your company's strengths and weaknesses by focusing on the performance drivers, that are to be derived from your company's own basic strategy. For example, if your company's overall philosophy emphasizes value-added creation and innovation, then the focus with regard to the value chain needs to be placed on R&D. If, on the other hand, you consider cost leadership to be of key importance, then you will want to focus on procurement and manufacturing.

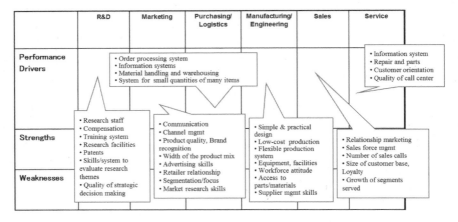

Figure 2.28.   Value chain.

Finally, clarifying the company's core competences makes it possible to develop new applications and new markets more effectively.

The three requirements for a core competence are as follows:

- Capabilities that facilitate access to a wider variety of markets.
- Capabilities that make an important contribution to the perceived customer benefits of the firm's end products.
- Capabilities with a low likelihood of being imitated by competitors.

As Hutt (2004) mentioned in his book, Honda's core competence in small engines is tied directly to important benefits sought by its customers: product reliability and fuel efficiency. Honda emphasizes these benefits in its marketing strategy across product lines: motorcycles, automobiles, generators, outboard engines, lawn mowers, snow blowers and aircrafts. Canon has become a strong competitor in various markets such as digital camera, image scanners, inkjet printers, laser printers, semiconductor lithography equipment, medical equipment, broad cast equipment, digital production printing systems, etc., based upon its core competences in precision mechanics, microelectronics, and fine optics.

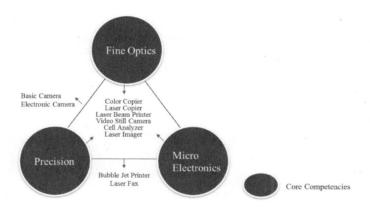

Source: Prahalad and Hamel (1990).

Figure 2.29.　Example — Canon's core competencies.

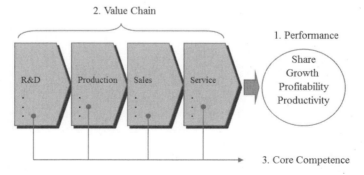

Figure 2.30.　Company analysis.

Macro Environment Analysis (Context)

The tools for macro environment analysis include politics, economy, society/culture, technology, environment/ecology and law/regulations, which are generally known as PESTEL. As mentioned before, PESTEL is called context, an important factor that is deeply rooted in society.

Table 2.1. Check list of macro environment factors (examples).

Evaluation Aspects	Evaluation Factors
Politics	Political system: democratic, authoritarian, dictatorial, frequency of government changes, frequency of riots, rebellions or strikes, military mobilization and influence, attitude to foreign companies, experts' evaluation on political stability.
Finance	Inflation, fluctuation in exchange rate, restrictions on capital flow, control over exchange rate, stability of exchange rate, foreign debt.
Economy	GDP per capita, income distribution (the top 20% income group to GDP ratio), annual growth rate of GDP, growth rate of agricultural population, growth rate of manufacturing population, growth rate of population in service industries, energy consumption, steel consumption.
Law	Restrictions on import and export (custom duties, allocation, restrictions on ownership, standards for products, regulations, restrictions on competition or monopolies, restrictions on pricing, environmental standards, regulations for patents and trademarks.
Demography	Population, average annual population growth rate, urbanization (urban population ratio), ratio of population aged from 0 to 14 years, population density, age structure of population, average longevity, infant mortality rate.

(Continued)

Table 2.1.   (*Continued*)

Evaluation Aspects	Evaluation Factors
Geography	Land area, topographical characteristics, climate conditions (average temperature), annual rainfall, and annual snowfall.
Technology	Technical skills, science level, manufacturing skills, adult literacy rate, PC ownership rate per capita, number of PhD graduates (social science, natural science), ratio of higher education graduates by age group, ratio of secondary education graduates by age group.
Society/Culture	Predominant values, lifestyle, racial mix, number of languages, population per doctor, main religion.
Network	Availability of communications and networks, railway networks (Km), road networks (Km), air freight (capacity), number of retail stores per capita, retail concentration, TV ownership rate, PC ownership rate, circulation of magazines and newspapers, number of mobile phones and smartphones per capita, number of cars per capita.
Basic resources/ Energy	Gas consumption, electric power consumption, electric power cost per kWh, energy consumption, monthly wage and salary costs, skill level of workers, possibility of obtaining capital, interest, and rent.
Sale and use of products	Sales volume of products, ownership rate of products (ratio of family-oriented businesses), increasing or decreasing trends of sales volume, purchase frequency, average purchase volume.
Use of complementary products and alternative products	Sales volume and growth rate of complementary products, user industry and its scale, sales volume and growth rate of alternative products, ownership of alternative products, market scale of used products.
Competition	Number of companies, main rival companies, growth rate of rival companies, market share, market share of top three companies.
Evaluation Aspects	Evaluation Factors.

Data: Adapted from Douglas and Craig (1983).

A detailed check list was shown previously. As for the interrelationship of the PESTEL elements of macro environment analysis, the effective use of newly-developed technology at the industry level brings new value to the customer market. While there are some cases where a negative aspect is demonstrated as being a side effect, it can be controlled or adjusted by politics and the law. Finally, technology is becoming established as a lifestyle, as well as a culture and society.

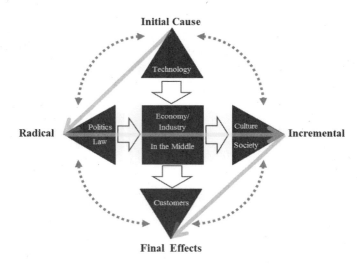

Data: Adapted from Kotler, Kartajaya, Huan (2006).

Figure 2.31. Context (PESTEL).

In the SWOT cross analysis, strategic options are extracted by applying the analysis of these 4Cs into the SWOT matrix and sorting them by S×O, W×O, S×T and W×T. This method is often used when implementing a project.

There are two points to keep in mind as a summary of the present state analysis.

The first point is that present state analysis is different from gathering information. The analysis is not about gathering just any piece of information, but rather the information should be gathered based on a hypothesis.

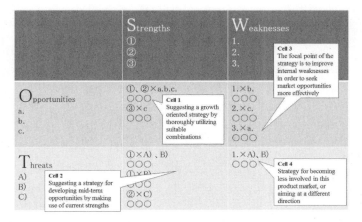

Figure 2.32.   Present state analysis (SWOT cross).

You need information in order to verify the validity of the strategic hypothesis that you already have.

The second point is that, as H. Igor Ansoff (father of strategic management) observed, management is decision-making under conditions of uncertainty and in partial ignorance. You should have the courage to make a decision with limited information. The door to opportunity is not open forever. Timing is very important. There is always something that cannot be worked out in detail. In this case, start small but think big. Then, scale up fast whenever possible, and modify flexibly as required.

2.2.3 *Business Goals: What Can You Achieve in Your Business within a Scheduled Period?*

The ideas for setting goals for business strategy are the same as those for corporate strategy. The market size, growth potential and competitive advantages of your company have been determined to a certain extent by the SWOT analysis. The sales potential of your company can be calculated using the following formula.

Market size × Growth rate × Share

You should set sales goals that are realistically achievable within a scheduled period and that are also concrete, taking into account the sales potential. It is often suggested that goal setting should be done according to the SMART criteria, which are:

- Specific
- Measurable
- Achievable
- Result-oriented
- Time-bound

In other words, goals should be set specifically, using numbers, within an achievable range, indicating results, and limiting a time frame. Another thing to mention concerning goal setting is BHAG (big, hairy, audacious goals), a phrase that is often heard in Silicon Valley in the United States. The idea is that BHAG may generate the energy of an exciting and challenging direction. Although this is a slightly different point of view, I will present it here for your reference.

Similar to goal setting for corporate strategy, if it is easy to forecast the future and if there is a high level of interaction with the environment, then the goal acts as a guideline for management that must be followed. It is also expected to play a role as the basis for control. On the other hand, if there is both a low level of environmental predictability and interaction with the environment, then the goal becomes a standard for considering a hypothesis through trial and error. In other words, it is expected to play a role as the basis for discussion to correct the original ideas and improve the strategy, and the highest priority should be given to flexibly responding to any change in the surroundings rather than to achieving the goal. It is important to take into account the environment where the business is conducted, and to consider the meaning of formulating a business strategy.

2.2.4 *Scope of Business*

The scope of business is often determined by factors such as the market (actual and potential customers), needs, products, technology, and solutions. The growth potential of a business greatly depends on how the scope of business is defined. In addition, the scope of business is an extremely important topic, as it has a significant influence over competitive strategy and marketing management, which will be discussed later. A scope of business that is too narrow limits potential chances, while a scope of business that is too broad can work well only with mass marketing, and subsequently this will diminish the meaning of strategic thinking. In general, the scope of business is defined by products and markets. In Figure 2.33, the X-axis shows customers/markets and the Y-axis shows products/solutions. This is called the product-market growth matrix. The product in the matrix should be interpreted as a list of solutions for customer needs. In other words, I would like to suggest that the scope of business should be defined by solutions for customer needs, such as personal mobility rather than a car, global network ability rather than a personal computer, or overall energy solutions rather than gas because solutions for customer needs would last forever as long as customers exist, but products tend to be obsoleted sooner or later.

		Market			
		I	II	III	IV
Product	A				
	B				
	C				
	D				

Figure 2.33.   Product-market growth matrix.

IBM has defined itself as a company offering global solutions for a small planet, and what IBM actually offers has also changed from ICT to solutions for business and industry. The high profitability of IBM is thought to be derived from its consulting and other range of services. Also, for a company selling copy machines, the profit structure of its business is supposed to be very different depending on the definition of its products, whether they are printers, printing services, document solutions, or information solutions.

The scope of business comprising of products to offer and markets to serve should be selected and determined mainly at the corporate strategy level. However, be sure to define it more in detail when formulating business strategy. In other words, the scope of business has a hierarchy in both products and markets. The following illustrates the layers in the scope of business.

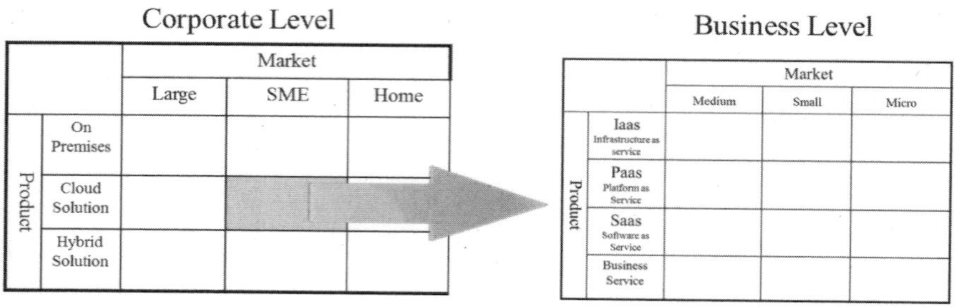

Hierarchy of Scope of Business

Level	Product	Market
Corporate	Product line	General Market
Business	Product	Special Market
Marketing	Value	Segment/Customer

Figure 2.34.   Product-market growth matrix.

As for defining the market, there are some cases where a single division deals with a group of an unspecified large number of customers including large-to-mid-sized and small-sized companies, as well as micro companies (Figure 2.35). On the other hand, many industrial material manufacturers, for example, deal with only a few specific customers. In this case, individual companies are regarded as a market; accordingly, the X-axis shows the names of those companies (Figure 2.36). Furthermore, there are more than a few companies that deal with only a single company (Figure 2.37). In this case, in order to explore business opportunities, it is beneficial that they divide that company into divisions and recognize each division as a market.

		Market			
		Large	Medium	Small	Micro
Product	Iaas Infrastructure as service				
	Paas Platform as Service				
	Saas Software as Service				
	Business Service				

Figure 2.35. The scope of business (for an unspecified large number of customers).

		Market			
		Apple	Cisco	Motorola	LG
Product	Devices				
	Modules				
	Systems				

Figure 2.36. The scope of business (for a few customers).

		Markets							
		Housing		Automobiles		Vessel		Aircraft	
		OEM	Tier1	OEM	Tier1	OEM	Tier1	OME	Tier1
Products	Engineering								
	Consulting								
	Maintenance								
	Operation								

Note: Tier 1 = first supplier to OEM (Original Equipment Manufacturer).

Figure 2.37.   The scope of business (for a single customer).

2.2.5 *Competitive Strategy: How to Compete to Achieve Your Goals*

After the scope of business has been clearly defined, the next step is to consider a strategy within the defined scope (products and markets), while also paying attention to the competition.

While the simple definition of business strategy is to consider methods to realize an achievable business goal that has been set based on the situation analysis, each business environment is different, and several options can be combined to create a method for achieving your goal. The individual state of each business should be understood, and then a specific solution should be determined. However, developing strategic options in a zero-base manner for all cases will require an enormous amount of time and cost. Therefore, in order to determine a specific solution, after understanding the basic direction, you should make a detailed observation of the situation where a specific problem has arisen. It is recommended to first have a good understanding of the basic theory on business strategy, including the conditions in which the theory is applied.

One of the simplest disciplines regarding how to develop competitive advantages in the face of competition is based upon the value to be created and provided to customers. There are two basic directions for the disciplines. One is differentiation. The goal of differentiation is to create a meaningful difference between your company and your competitors through product innovation. The other one is cost leadership, the goal of which is to create the same benefit for a lower price through process innovation. The following shows superior value configurations compared to an average competitor.

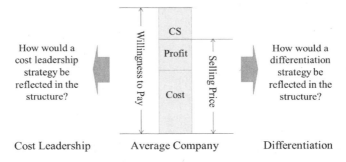

Figure 2.38.   Two directions for competitive strategy.

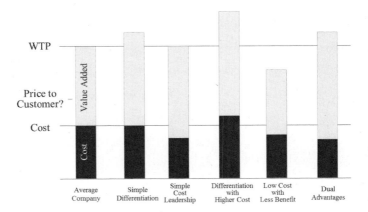

Figure 2.39.   Superior value configurations compared to an average competitor.

Porter's model and Kotler's model are types of competitive strategy. Michael Porter's model consists of two factors: whether the competitive advantages involve cost (proposed solution is homogeneous) or differentiation (proposed solution is heterogeneous), and whether the target is concentrated (avoiding competition) or broad (accepting competition).

Source: Porter (1982).

Figure 2.40. Model proposed by Michael Porter (strategy types based on competitive advantage).

Way of Competition / Attitude of Competition	Heterogeneity	Homogeneity
Accepting competition	Differentiation	Cost Leadership
Avoiding competition	Focused Differentiation	Cost Focus

Source: Amended from Porter's model.

Figure 2.41.   Strategy types based on competitive advantage.

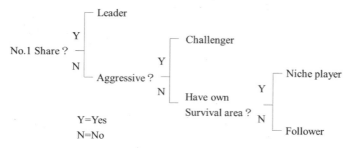

Figure 2.42.   Model proposed by Philip Kotler (strategy types based on competitive position).

Kotler's model has four types: leader, challenger, niche player and follower. Each of these four types is shown and the basic directions are described.

More specifically, which strategy should be used for what kind of situation? Cost leadership in Michael Porter's model is a strategy, which industry-leaders (companies that are number one in share) are more likely to use. In addition to decreasing the fixed costs due to economies of scale, the more the cumulative production amount, the more the variable costs decrease due to the experience curve effect. For example, the more experience you have, the more sophisticated you become in operations for procurement and production, resulting in low cost purchases and less inferior and defective products. So the companies that have secured top share can reduce costs. The basic strategy of top companies is not to decrease the price drastically despite having low costs; rather it is to maximize their share while ensuring a certain level of margin.

The competitive strategy for companies that are number two or lower in the industry should be something other than cost leadership, which is mentioned above. That means it is either a differentiation strategy or a focus strategy. A differentiation strategy is basically targeting a broad market and differentiating the products or services from those of the leader company. In other words, it is aimed at attracting customers by offering a benefit different from that of the leader company.

Conversely, a focus strategy does not compete directly with the leader, but rather the focus is on concentrating business resources on a specific customer market that is different from the leader's market. As the strategy for targeting the entire market responds to the whole target market in the same manner, a niche market with unmet needs is likely to arise. A focus strategy is to create new value by targeting a niche market.

A focus strategy is divided further into a cost focus strategy in which a company competes on cost performance, and a focused differentiation strategy whereby a company pursues differentiation. If it is possible to create an original space in the market where major companies cannot enter, a company should utilize its original core competencies and promote a focused differentiation strategy to respond to needs at a higher level, by differentiating thoroughly in a narrow market. If such an original space does not exist, then a company should consider a cost focus strategy by providing downscaled products with a focus on price-sensitive markets.

Kotler (Competitive Position)	Leaders	Challengers	Niche player	Followers
Porter(Basic Direction)	Cost Leadership	Differentiation	Focused Differentiation	Cost Focus
Basic Strategy	·Marketing in all directions ·Homogenizing with what challengers do	·Promoting differentiation against the leader through semi-coverage	·Total solutions to a limited segment or niche market	·Downscale product to price-sensitive market

Source: Amended from Porter's model and Kotler's model.

Figure 2.43. Types of competitive strategy (correlation between Porter and Kotler).

2.2.6 *Marketing Management: How to Create Solutions to Customer Needs*

R. J. Dolan (1997) made the following comment about marketing.

> Marketing is the process via which a firm creates value for its chosen customers. Value is created by meeting customer needs. Marketing strategy can be regarded as a plan for creating value through the above process.

In this book, marketing is defined as the process in which value is created by finding and defining the unmet needs of customers and providing unique solutions to them. The process for formulating a marketing strategy can be divided into the following two major activities:

(1) Selecting a target market and determining the desired positioning of what to offer in the minds of the target customers
(2) Specifying a plan for the marketing activities to achieve the desired positioning.

The first part is to be processed through STP (segmentation, targeting, and positioning). "S" stands for segmentation, which is to divide the market into homogenous groups that respond differently from other groups to the offerings. "T" represents targeting, which means selecting a couple of attractive groups within those groups, while also defining the hypothetical needs of those customers. "P" stands for positioning, which is to determine the desired positioning of what to offer in the minds of the target customers. Through this process, companies can clarify the basic concept of which benefits (products, services and solutions) to propose for meeting what kind of needs for which type of customers/markets.

The second process is for realizing the abovementioned concept, and consists of a series of activities such as developing and designing the benefits to offer (product), expressing the value of what to offer (price), drawing up and managing sales channels and distributions of what to offer (place), and conveying information and stimulation about what to offer (promotion). The set of above mentioned 4Ps is also called the marketing mix. Building a marketing mix comprising of the 4Ps can be considered as the process for designing, expressing, delivering, and communicating the benefits of what to offer, which have been defined by positioning.

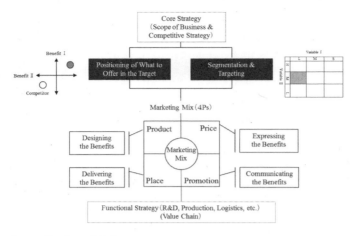

Source: Kasahara (2013).

Figure 2.44. Marketing management integration of targeting and positioning.

Contingent Approach to Market Conditions

Marketing styles have been shifting from mass marketing to one-to-one marketing; this has been supported by technological developments in recent years, as markets are becoming more sophisticated and mature. Actually, a wide variety of choices and customized service options have been quite useful in differentiating from competitors in markets where customers have different and unique needs. An important issue in marketing decisions is to decide the extent to which there should be customization for each customer. The following points should be considered for selecting an appropriate marketing approach:

Customer distribution: Concentrated (limited number of large customers) vs. diverse (many small customers)

Needs quality: Homogeneous (similar needs) vs. heterogeneous (different needs)

If your business is situated in the upper-left area of Figure 2.45, where a large number of customers with similar needs exist, mass marketing would be an appropriate approach. In mass marketing, the process is simple; simply consider the market as a collection of customers who have homogeneous needs and prepare only one kind of positioning, and the set the marketing mix based on the positioning. If your business is in the lower-right area, where you have only a limited number of large sized customers who have unique needs, you should apply one-to-one marketing, which is to create unique solutions to each customer. For the upper-right area that comprises a relatively large number of customers who have different needs, segmentation marketing, which is to be proceeded through STP would be the appropriate approach.

The basic step in each style is as follows:

Segmentation marketing: Segmentation→Targeting→ Positioning+4Ps

One-to-one marketing: Targeting→Positioning+4Ps

Mass marketing: Positioning+4Ps

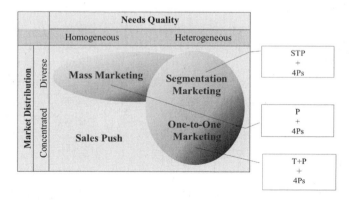

Source: Kasahara (2009).

Figure 2.45. Marketing approach based upon market distribution and needs quality.

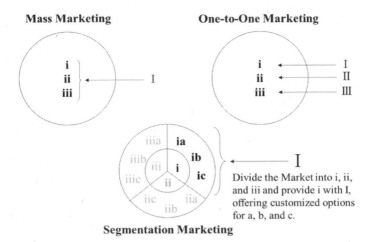

Figure 2.46.   Basic marketing styles.

Segmentation Marketing for Many Customers with Different Needs

As an example of a segmentation marketing approach for many customers with different needs, let me introduce an SPT process applied for Southwest Airlines Co., which is a major U.S. airlines and the world's largest low-cost carrier, headquartered in Dallas, Texas. The company was established in 1967 and adopted its current name in 1971. Southwest Airlines has mainly operated Boeing 737s, and as of August 2012, it was the largest airline operator of the 737 worldwide. As of April 2014, Southwest Airlines operates scheduled services to 89 destinations in 42 states and Puerto Rico, the newest being Pensacola, Florida, Memphis, Tennessee, and Richmond, Virginia, as of November 3, 2013.

Southwest did not use the more traditional "hub and spoke" flight routing system that most other major airlines used, preferring the "Point to Point" system instead, and it has notably large operations in certain airports. Approximately, 80% of Southwest passengers are local passengers, meaning only 20% of that passengers are connecting passengers. This is significantly higher than most airlines, where passengers often connect in hub cities. The main target segment consists of business and frequent travelers. Southwest's competitive strategy combines a high level of employee and aircraft productivity with low unit costs by reducing aircraft turnaround time, particularly at the gate. It is famous for its friendly atmosphere to entertain travelers, and in fact, entertaining performances such as costume contests, bingo games, and karaoke are sometimes provided during flights.

As part of its effort to control costs, Southwest sometimes uses secondary airports in cities. Secondary airports normally have lower costs, and may be more convenient for travelers than major airports in the same destinations. For example, Southwest flies to Chicago-Midway instead of Chicago-O'Hare, with an average of six flights per day.

Southwest maintains excellent customer satisfaction ratings. According to the Department of Transportation (DOT), for many years Southwest has ranked number one among all U.S. airlines in terms of fewest customer complaints. It has consistently received the lowest ratio of complaints per passengers boarded among all major U.S. carriers that have been reporting statistics to the DOT since September 1987, which is when the DOT began tracking customer satisfaction statistics and publishing its Air Travel Consumer Report.

The first step of STP is segmentation, which is to identify customer groups that respond differently from other groups to your offerings. It is useful to clarify the hypothetical needs or key buying factors (KBFs) of those customers in each group. The most useful segment-defining variables for an offering are rarely obvious. To avoid missing a useful way of defining segments, it is important to consider a wide range of variables. Some of the frequently used variables are:

- Demographics: Age, Income, Occupation, Sex.
- Geographic: Country, Region, Urban vs. Rural.
- Psychographic: Lifestyle Level of Involvement.

- User Status: User, Nonuser.
- Buying Behavior: Heavy, Medium, Light, None.

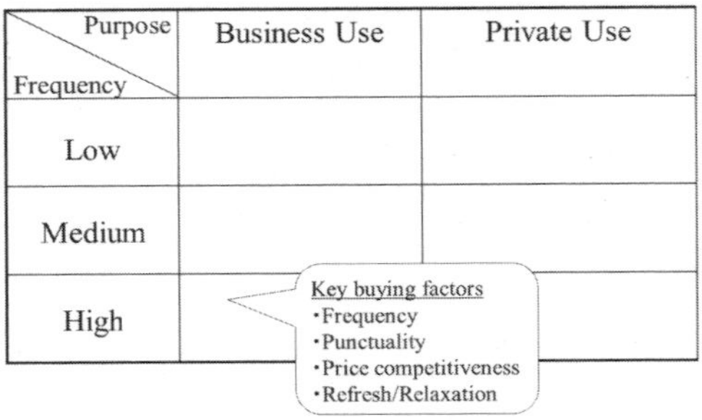

Purpose / Frequency	Business Use	Private Use
Low		
Medium		
High	Key buying factors • Frequency • Punctuality • Price competitiveness • Refresh/Relaxation	

Figure 2.47. Segmentation for the case of Southwest Airlines.

The next step is targeting, which is to select a couple of attractive groups in the market, based upon external attractiveness and internal fitness such as the resources' fit with the KBFs.

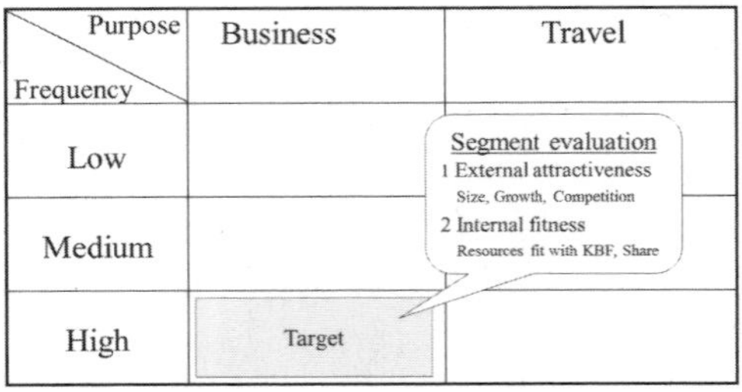

Purpose / Frequency	Business	Travel
Low		Segment evaluation 1 External attractiveness Size, Growth, Competition 2 Internal fitness Resources fit with KBF, Share
Medium		
High	Target	

Figure 2.48. Targeting for the case of Southwest Airlines.

When deploying the above STP+4Ps, in addition to the already completed situation analysis, it is recommended to add further new investigations and analyses as required during implementation. Do the needs of the customer market selected as the target really exist? If so, how strong are those needs? What is the order of the key buying factors? What is the scale of the customer market? Companies should consider formulating some methods for answering these types of questions. Listening to the

■Points in Evaluation for Targeting

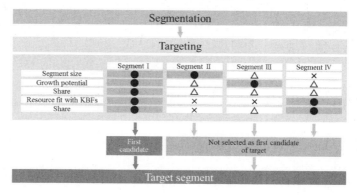

Figure 2.49.   Targeting assessment.

real views of target customers (at the very least) using focus groups, interviews, questionnaire-based surveys, ethnographic approach, and other types of investigations to verify the hypothetical strategy is essential for checking if these hypotheses are on the right track. Below is a brief introduction of a customer satisfaction survey for verifying the needs hypotheses of the target segments. The process is as follows:

(1) Determine the survey outline: clarify the purpose of the survey, its targets and sample size, and survey methods, etc.
(2) Set the hypothesis: conduct pre-research and formulate the survey hypothesis
(3) Design the questionnaire: write up the question items and determine an assessment scale (five or seven levels, etc.)
(4) Sample extraction: determine the segments as survey targets and extract a sample
(5) Conduct the survey: carry out the survey, after doing a trial run to ensure there are no problems
(6) Tabulation and analysis of the questionnaire: download the survey results into an Excel sheet, and arrange and analyze the data

When designing the questionnaire, make sure to include dependent variables, such as overall satisfaction and intent to repurchase and recommend to others. A dependent variable is a symbol that is expected to be explained or influenced by the independent or explanatory variables. An independent variable is a symbol over which the researcher has some control, and that is hypothesized to cause or influence the dependent variable. The dependent variables are broken down into QCDS (quality, cost, delivery, development, design, and service or the 4Ps (product, price, place, and promotion) and the survey is rolled out on a MECE (mutually exclusive and collectively exhaustive) basis.

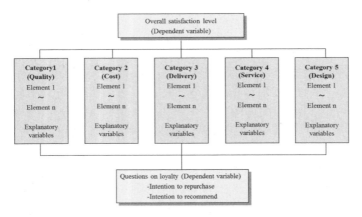

Figure 2.50.   Sample structure of a survey.

The Figure below is an image of a customer satisfaction survey. The items are divided into broad categories within the framework, and then broken down into smaller questions. The basic stance is determined according to the level of satisfaction and degree of importance of each item; however, areas with a high degree of importance and a low level of satisfaction require focused improvement. Conversely, areas with a low degree of importance and a high level of satisfaction are an over-specification and the excess should be cut. In contrast, areas with both a high degree of importance and a high level of satisfaction should be maintained, while areas with both a low degree of importance and a low level of satisfaction should be left disregarded.

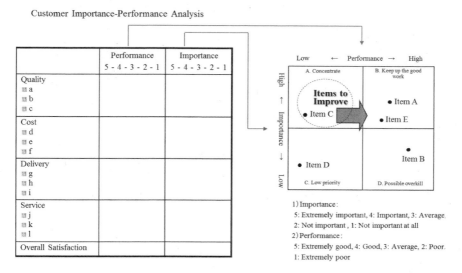

Figure 2.51.   Sample of customer satisfaction survey.

Positioning means to determine the desired positioning of what to offer in the minds of the target customers. Through this process, companies can clarify the basic concept of which benefits (products, services and solutions) to propose for meeting what kind of needs for which type of markets/customers. The positioning process begins by identifying the relevant set of competing solutions and defining the attributes that are critical to determine which product the customers like. The next step is to gather information from the customers about their ratings of each product, followed by determining the product's current position versus those of competing offerings. The final step is to examine the fit between preferences of the target customers and the current positing of the products:

(1) Identify the relevant set of products
(2) Identify the set of determinant attributes that customers use to decide their preferred choice

(3) Gather information from existing and potential customers about their ratings of each product based on the determinant attributes
(4) Determine the product's current position versus competing offerings for the target segment
(5) Examine the fit between the preferences of the target segment and the current position of the products
(6) Select the positioning or repositioning strategy

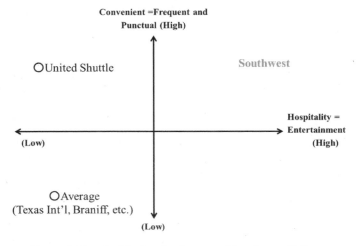

Figure 2.52.   Positioning for the case of Southwest Airlines.

The marketing mix of Southwest Airlines, which is aimed at realizing the positioning in Figure 2.52, can be explained by the following:

(a) Product
  (i) Frequency, accuracy, safety
  (ii) Casual atmosphere
  (iii) Friendly entertainment
  (iv) No in-flight meals, pay-for services
  (v) Domestic routes only
  (vi) Short-haul flights

(b) Price
  (i)   Low-cost fare

(c) Place
   (i) Direct reservation through e-tickets.

(d) Promotion
   (i) Friendly and fun message
   (ii) CEO as a image character

(e) Low cost operations
   (i) Crew/Cabin attendants also clean the insides of the plane
   (ii) Only Boeing 737 planes
   (iii) Point-to-point
   (iv) 15-minute turnaround (Departure preparations)
   (v) Use of small airfields

One-to-One Marketing for a Limited Number of Customers with Different Needs

The first step for one-to-one marketing for a limited number of customers with different needs is to prioritize and select certain customers based upon the customer attractiveness and competitive position of your company in each customer. Customer attractiveness includes the size of the business, volume of purchasing, R&D level, share in the industry, expected future growth rate, financial conditions, etc. Competitive position in each customer indicates how much share your company has in the total procurement of the category in the customer. The second step is to identify the buying center or decision making unit (DMU) of the targeted customer and to determine the needs of each member in the buying center. The third step is to confirm the buying process of the customer. The major stages of the organizational buying process are illustrated in Figure 2.56. By considering what will happen on each stage, we need to prepare for our marketing and sales activities. The fourth step is to clarify forces influencing organizational behavior such as the environmental factors of the customer (economic outlook, technological change, trade regulations), strategic factors (goals, scope of business, competitive strategy, organizational positioning of purchasing), group factors (roles, relative influence, and patterns of interaction of buying decision, and supplier evaluation criteria), and individual factors (job function, past experience, and buying motives of individual members). The final step is to develop the conceptual positioning of the proposed solutions in the target customers.

(1) Prioritize and select certain customers based upon customer attractiveness and competitive position in each customer
(2) Identify the buying center of each customer and determine the needs of each member in the buying center
(3) Confirm the buying process from problem recognition to performance review
(4) Clarify organizational buying behavior based upon influencing forces
(5) Develop the conceptual positioning of the proposed solutions in the target customers

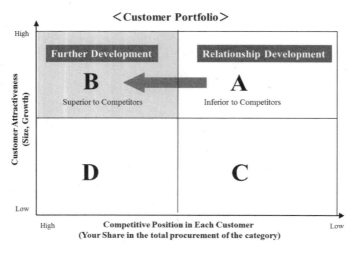

Figure 2.53.   Focusing on customers with high potential.

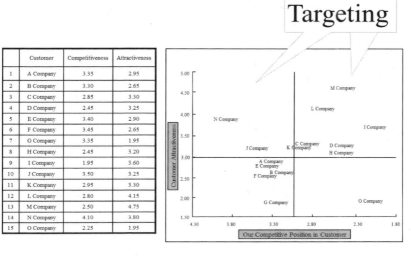

	Customer	Competitiveness	Attractiveness
1	A Company	3.35	2.95
2	B Company	3.30	2.65
3	C Company	2.85	3.30
4	D Company	2.45	3.25
5	E Company	3.40	2.90
6	F Company	3.45	2.65
7	G Company	3.35	1.95
8	H Company	2.45	3.20
9	I Company	1.95	3.60
10	J Company	3.50	3.25
11	K Company	2.95	3.30
12	L Company	2.80	4.15
13	M Company	2.50	4.75
14	N Company	4.10	3.80
15	O Company	2.25	1.95

Figure 2.54.   Customer portfolio (example).

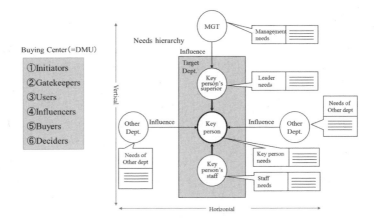

Figure 2.55.   Buying center/DMU.

Marketing Mix

A marketing mix, as a set of activities to achieve the desired positioning, is designed using the 4Ps, namely, product, price, place, and promotion. I will now discuss the key points of each element.

1. Problem recognition
2. General description of need
3. Product specification
4. Supplier search
5. Acquisition and analysis of proposals
6. Supplier selection
7. Selection of order routine
8. Performance review

Figure 2.56.   Major stages of the organizational buying process.

Product

A product is an item that is in a form whereby its benefits can be consumed by a customer.

For example, what is the benefit of Microsoft products? Simply put, it is making various kinds of work more efficient. This benefit is assisted by a basic OS and fundamental applications as actual products, and is generally called naked solutions. These are commonly considered as being physical products, but are not referred to as products in marketing. In order to truly enhance the efficiency of numerous work duties, the customer requires options and tasks to realize cost reductions and facilitate improvements in carrying out work. So Microsoft products are regarded as items that also include these options, as well as a range of services for improving the ICT skills of companies.

Next, let's look at the case of Starbucks. What is the benefit of Starbucks? In a word, it's being a third place. It's neither your home nor office, but rather another (third) place where you can relax. The physical products used to realize this benefit include delicious premium coffee and a well-styled and inviting store interior. However, these products alone are not sufficient for producing the benefit of a place to relax. A sophisticated selection of BGM (background music), good-looking baristas who make and serve the coffee, interaction with friendly staff, a non-smoking area, and other elements blend together to create for the first time the third place that is Starbucks in a form that customers can consume.

Product of Starbucks

【Third Place: Experience for relaxation】
➢ The core benefit that the customer derives from using the product

【Relaxing interior, premium coffee】
➢ Physical and performance attributes of the product

【Sophisticated BGM, good looking baristas, non-smoking service】
➢ Various services provided with the physical products

Figure 2.57.   Product (B2C).

ABB Power Plants

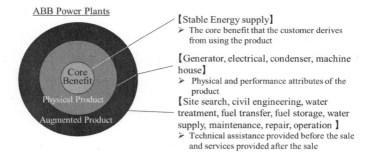

【Stable Energy supply】
➢ The core benefit that the customer derives from using the product

【Generator, electrical, condenser, machine house】
➢ Physical and performance attributes of the product

【Site search, civil engineering, water treatment, fuel transfer, fuel storage, water supply, maintenance, repair, operation 】
➢ Technical assistance provided before the sale and services provided after the sale

Figure 2.58.   Product (B2B).

We may see some measures emerge for products that include essential services to realize these benefits, even in industries with tough demands from customers for cost cutting because of commoditization.

Lastly, let's consider the example of industrial products. For instance, what are the products of a company that manufactures and sells gas turbines? First, we shall consider the proposed benefit. Looking at it simply, the benefit is most likely the production of energy, abbreviated as energy creation. It is not enough to just make gas turbines as products in order to provide energy from the earth. Prior to purchasing a gas turbine, energy companies, which are the customers, will first carry out a series of technical reviews, and then hold various meetings and work on raising funds. At the same time, they will also create an enormous amount of documents for internal circulation and review as they proceed with the project. Other essential post-purchasing tasks include installing the turbine and working on the MRO (maintenance, repair and operation). So what if companies were to provide services to help reduce the customer's internal workload? When such services are made available, the physical product of a gas turbine will be able to achieve its effect of energy creation for the first time. To reiterate, a product is an item that is in a form whereby the customer is able to consume its benefit.

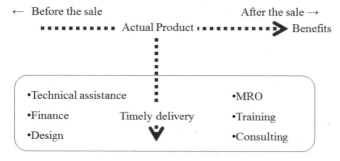

Figure 2.59.   Product as total package of benefits.

Price

When setting the price of a product or service, companies must consider at least three things: customer value, the company's cost of goods, and competitor prices. Customer value refers to the ratio of the extent of the obtainable benefit from the products and services the customer is considering purchasing, and the amount of the cost the customer has to pay in order to obtain the benefit.

$$\text{Customer value} = \text{Benefit/Cost}$$

Benefits include: (1) rational benefit and emotional benefit, and (2) functional and operational benefit. Cost includes (1) acquisition cost, storage cost, usage cost, and disposal cost, and (2) economic cost, time cost, energy cost, and mental stress cost. Price setting as described in textbooks is a general determination of price by referring to the price range of competitors, with customer value set as the upper limit and company costs set as the lower limit. However, companies need to be aware that there is a possibility of the customer's perceived price dropping if competitors' prices are extremely low. In that case, companies need to make every effort to objectively validate the price from the customer's perspective, while eventually setting the price in the range of the customer's perceived price level.

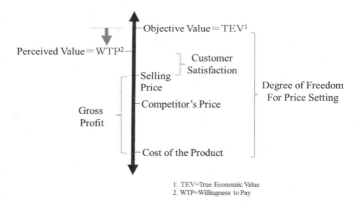

1: TEV=True Economic Value
2. WTP=Willingness to Pay

Figure 2.60.   Price setting perspective.

There are two approaches to pricing new products: skimming pricing policy, and the market penetration pricing policy. The skimming pricing policy involves setting a high price to reap profits in the early stages. It is ideal for products with relatively long-lasting competitiveness and a steady demand curve over the long term.

On the other hand, the market penetration pricing policy works well if the threat of competition is looming large, and there are conditions that allow for a considerable fall in costs by expanding production quantity, by which after setting a low price and winning a large share of the market, the company can establish its superiority in cost competition through economies of scale and the experience curve effect, and over time secure sizeable profits. The applicability of the market penetration pricing policy is positively correlated to the market's future growth potential (i.e. the higher the potential growth, the greater the applicability).

Lastly, in this section on price, I will summarize methods for responding to the threat of competitors' price reduction. Basically, companies should always try to not join in any competition that cannot be won, and fight it out only in areas where they have a competitive strength, while avoiding any battles that are clearly disadvantageous. Let's assume a company lowers its price to counter a competitor's price cut; in this case, it should consider whether the competitor has the will and ability to recover the price gap. If they don't, then the company can embark on a price battle. However, any company engaging in price competition needs to be aware of the strong possibility that its competitors may retaliate, and the cost of measures to protect against this could be higher than any negatives that may arise due to a loss of market share. As long as there are no adverse effects on other markets, companies should focus on maximizing long-term profits and not join in any short-term price wars with competitors.

Place (Sales Channel)

There are two key themes concerning place for sales channels within marketing strategy. The first is designing an optimal sales channel for achieving the marketing goal. This is no easy task. There are an infinite number of choices for sales channels, and many target segments will require the concurrent use of multiple ones. The structure of these channels also needs to be regularly reviewed in light of the ever-changing environment. The changing needs of customers, the rapid growth of e-commerce, and numerous other factors suggest the need for an innovative sales channel strategy.

The second theme is that these sales channels designed to meet set goals must be managed. Effectively managing sales channel activities requires a company to select the channel partners, provide incentives for achieving the desired performance, smooth out any conflicts between members, develop performance assessment methods, and so on.

First, I will introduce the process for designing a sales channel.

(1) Select and define the target customer segments
(2) Ascertain target customers' channel requirements by segments
(3) Assess your current competency in satisfying the needs of targeted customers
(4) Investigate the channel policies of competitors, and use them as a reference for making improvements
(5) Design channels based on a combination of both direct and indirect sales
(6) Evaluate the channels and make structural adjustments as required

Designing a sales channel can be simply described by creating the structural chart shown below. The first step is deciding whether to use direct or indirect sales, or a combination of the two, and whether to add e-commerce. The second step is determining the number of layers; will it be the three layers of manufacturer-wholesaler-retailer, or will the wholesaler and retailer layers be omitted, or will the two-layer approach of manufacturer-wholesaler be used? Lastly, what type of business will be used at each layer, and how many? These are some of the factors that need to be considered.

The two basic points to consider when formulating a sales channel are reach (the number of target customers and their physical distribution), and richness (the complexity of communication required for both incorporating

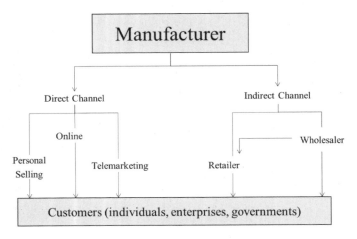

Figure 2.61.   Channel structure.

customer needs and creating customer-targeted proposals). If the customer reach extends to the far ends of the channel but richness is extremely low, then e-commerce should be selected. If the customer reach is narrow but richness is high, then direct sales is preferable, while indirect sales would suit a medium level of customer reach and richness.

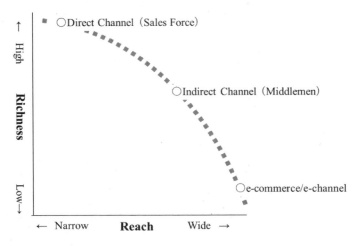

Source: Author's lecture notes.

Figure 2.62.   Reach (quantity) vs. richness (quality).

Lastly, I will discuss the management of sales channels. Even if a company has set up a strategically ideal sales channel structure, it cannot be fully functional unless the company provides incentives for the channel members. Companies need to recognize that a sales channel is a partnership between members. If manufacturing companies and distributors work together in a partnership and the manufacturing companies can provide specialist knowledge and support to the distributors, it will raise the overall effectiveness of the sales channel.

Much empirical research has highlighted the following as valuable and useful methods for realizing a functional sales channel: award systems, product training, goal sharing, constructive feedback, formulating annual plans through collaboration and regularly assessing the achievement rate, holding meetings for information sharing between members, and so on. Distributor meetings can lead to extremely significant results, depending on how they are used. In the case of a company I was able to actually observe in person, the proposals from channel members are summarized by the manufacturing company, while the programs for actual implementation are selected and presented in a report that is distributed to members of the meeting. Most of the proposals are in fact implemented, and this helps maintain a high level of motivation among distributors.

Finally, I will present an excerpt from the book "Channel Champions" by Steven Wheeler and Evan Hirsh.

A sales channel is the point where customers and companies intersect. It involves everything relating to the place and method of purchasing and using products and services. The sales channel is the route by which companies reach their customers, and is essentially an ongoing relationship with the customer; therefore, when considering sales channels, it is essential to look at an overall strategy. Effective management of sales channels goes beyond a single company, and it has the potential to rebuild an entire industry.

Promotion

Promotion is the appropriate set of ways to communicate with customers so as to foster an awareness of what to offer, acquire knowledge about it, generate a positive attitude towards it, and create an intention to purchase it. Promotion can be divided into five categories: advertisement, public relations, personal selling, sales promotion, and direct marketing. Effective marketing requires integrated communications combining the above.

An advertisement is a pay-for information communication activity by which a company promotes itself or its products and services using non-personal media (e.g. television, newspapers, magazines, etc.).

Public relations (PR) is referred to as non-paid communication by non-personal media, and is used to distribute information about a company's image and individual products and services through a third party other than sellers. It often involves using articles written about the company's products.

Meanwhile, personal selling, as the name states, uses the personal media of person-to-person interaction to communicate the desired message, make presentations, answer questions, secure orders, and so forth.

Sales promotion is a category that encompasses everything other than the activities that fall within the above three categories. It collectively means the testing of products and services and the provisions of various short-term incentives for encouraging purchasing, and includes sampling, prizes, rebates, allowances, coupons, contest, low-interest financing, exhibitions or trade shows, demonstration, and so on.

To finish, I will discuss direct marketing, which is gaining attention these days. Specifically, it refers to using LinkedIn, Facebook, YouTube, the Web, email and related media to directly communicate with current customers and potential customers and also obtain a direct response from them. As you have probably already noticed, sales promotion (broadly defined) is classified based on the rather vague principles of categorization. Although, this ambiguity is also probably one of the strengths of marketing.

I have touched on the categories of sales promotion, and now I will look at how these categories should be determined.

Let's use some aspects of the consumer behaviour theory to consider the above question. The following is a process-based model of the purchasing behaviour of individual customers when making a decision.

Stage 1 Recognizing problems and needs

Recognition of a gap between your current and desired state, and the need to resolve any problems you may have. Or, having the feeling of not being satisfied.

Stage 2 Searching for suppliers

Collecting information on products or suppliers that could resolve any problems.

Stage 3 Evaluating the purchasing alternatives that comprise products, brands, solutions, or suppliers

Evaluating purchasing alternatives based on information obtained in the information search stage using certain criteria.

Stage 4 Selecting and purchasing

Going to a store or dealer to make a purchase.

Stage 5 Post-purchase review

Assessing your satisfaction or dissatisfaction after purchasing and actually using the product. Also, re-evaluating the alternatives for selection.

The customer's mind changes during the course of this purchasing process. First, through searching for information, the customer becomes aware of previously unknown products and services. In other words, they recognize and also properly understand the characteristics of these products and services, thus enabling them to determine their attitude if they like or dislike the product, and then form an intent to buy, that leads to an actual purchase. Integrating these psychological changes with the decision-making process described earlier produces the following chart.

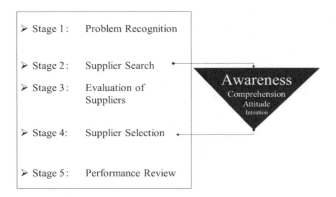

Figure 2.63. Purchasing as a decision making process.

So what is the best approach in a situation as depicted in the following chart? Let's consider some specific promotions that may be applicable here.

	【Case A】	【Case B】	【Case C】
	100	100	100
Awareness	42	80	71
Comprehension	29	70	58
Attitude	22	16	40
Intention	15	12	14
Purchase	10	10	10

Figure 2.64. How would you raise the purchase rate?

Case A is quite simple. As the recognition or awareness level is low, the preferred approach would be rolling out advertisements for making the products and services

more widely known. But what about Case B? This is somewhat more complex, as the recognition level is high and
the products and services are well understood. Moreover,
the customers have decided they don't like them. In this
case, the company should either accept that it needs to
review the product concept entirely, or better still try to
change the target.

And what about Case C? The scores are fairly reasonable up until attitude, but the company didn't score high
enough is confidence for a purchase. Even though the
customer thinks the products and services are good, it's
does not provide enough motivation for making a purchase.
In this situation, as a sales promotion activity, I would
recommend doing something to get the attention of the
customer and boost their interest. For instance, a company
that sells large equipment could perhaps hold a demonstration of the product as part of a factory tour, or offer a
small device on a trial basis. A company selling consumable
products could provide samples to customers, or preferably
offer a special discount for a limited time as a price incentive, or add a low-interest financing option.

In short, attitude is the key. If a customer says that
your products and services are good, using some form of
promotion should work. So, how do customers form their
attitudes (like/dislike, it's good, etc.)?

$$\text{Attitude} = \sum_{i=1}^{n} b_i e_i$$

Attitude is expressed as in the formula above.
Basically, there are multiple target products and services
with a limited number (n) of attributes for comparative
review. If a candidate target product has all the features
the customer requires regarding a certain attribute, it is
given a +3, and if there are no such features, it is given a
−3. Whether or not these features are present is expressed
by a belief (b). How each attribute is originally evaluated
is expressed by (e) — that is, +3 if having the attribute is

favorable and −3 if it isn't — indicating its level of importance. This formula determines the customer's attitude by summing the belief and importance of each attribute.

Where:

b_i is the belief that the target product has an i-ranked attribute;

e_i is the evaluative aspects of an i-ranked attribute, and level of importance of b_i;

n is the number of relevant beliefs for that person;

Attitude is the sum of the numbers obtained by multiplying the belief (possession level) and evaluation (importance level) of each attributes of the product.

Attribute	Evaluation e (+3 if having the attribute is favorable and -3 if it isn't – indicates its level of importance)	Belief about attribute b (likely present +3, likely absent -3)					
		Company A (Fast work)		Company B (Low cost)		Company C (Good quality)	
Quality	+3	+1	+3	−1	−3	+3	+9
Cost	−1	+1	−1	+3	−3	−3	+3
Delivery	+2	+3	+6	+1	+2	+1	+2
Total			+8		−4		+14

Figure 2.65. Mechanisms for shaping attitudes: what is the possession level (belief) of each attribute and its evaluation (importance level)?

Lastly, I will comment on the steps for formulating a sales promotion strategy in a broad sense, based on the following six Ms.

(1) Confirming the purpose of the promotion (Mission)
(2) Setting the market (Market)
(3) Determining the promotion budget (Money)
(4) Creating messages (Message)
(5) Selecting media (Media)
(6) Checking the effectiveness of the promotion (Measurement)

In terms of advertising, the steps are as follows: (1) Confirming the purpose of the advertisement; (2) Clarifying the target and audience; (3) Determining the advertising budget; (4) Creating messages (benefit required by the target customers, clarifying the needs of members comprising the buying center); (5) Selecting media (horizontal/vertical type, delivery costs, frequency); and (6) Checking the effectiveness of the advertisement (checking the achievement rate).

Current Issues in Marketing Management

So far we've looked at general theories of marketing management; what I'd like to comment on now is not so much an advanced application of these theories, but a theme that should be kept in mind — how to avoid commoditization. I was consulted by a long-standing corporate client about a recent trend in deteriorating profits due to product commoditization.

Why does commoditization occur in the first place? It is regarded as a situation when there are difficulties in differentiating products and services, making it hard for even customers to find any differences in essential components ("commodity" originally refers to raw materials). Actually, this corporate client tried to differentiate the number of pixels of its image processing system from 5 million to 10 million. However, the customers weren't able to fully recognize this difference and it was not reflected in the price. The only result of this effort to differentiate was that some customers felt the product had been over-engineered.

So what is an effective marketing strategy for companies to persue in the present day, where successful differentiation has become extremely tough? Figure 2.66 is a springboard for considering how to avoid the commodity trap.

The Y-axis in the figure represents the benefits to offer, consisting of functional benefits (processing speed, capacity, thinness, lightness, compactness, durability, etc.) and emotional benefits (stimulus to the five senses, such as usability and cool design, and also peace of mind, warmth, and excitement). The X-axis represents how to deliver these benefits, and whether only a hard-centered approach will be used or if soft elements will also be added.

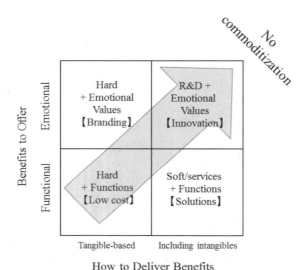

Source: Adapted from Narayandas (2003), and Nobeoka (2006).

Figure 2.66.   How to avoid commoditization (proposed benefits and format to deliver the benefits).

The bottom left box shows a hard-centered roll out of functional benefits. A typical example of this in PC brands is Dell. In this area, new products are quickly copied through reverse engineering. Consequently, mechanisms for providing products at a low cost are essential. Let's look at Dell's classic business model, which is a combination of direct sales and order-based production or build-to-order. The company receives a customer order and procures parts and devices from external suppliers, as per the request.

The customized products are then sold directly to the customer, bypassing retailers. Direct sales enable Dell to omit the channel margin, and its build-to-order production system results in a high inventory turnover. Moreover, the price of semiconductor parts and devices falls daily and even more advanced parts are delivered to the market in a swift cycle, which means that any drop in the price of parts and devices can be immediately reflected in the product price. As a result, customers are able to purchase a computer with the latest and still up-to-date specifications at a low cost. The point of this quadrant is how to sustain and expand a competitive advantage in a commoditized market, rather than opting for no commoditization.

One approach of no commoditization is promoting emotional benefits. This refers to demonstrating the product's sensory values of stimulus to the five senses, such as usability and cool design, and also peace of mind, warmth, and excitement. In PC products, this is illustrated in Panasonic's tough book and tough pad series. As the name suggests, these are durable products that can function well in any type of tough environment, thus providing peace of mind to the target customers such as construction workers, police, and special brigades. The point of this quadrant is branding a product as a hard element.

The next approach of no commoditization is rolling out hard elements with various services and soft elements added.

This is going back in time somewhat, but computer communication companies such as Nifty Serve, developed and run by Fujitsu, is a classic case of combining the hard element of PCs with communication services. Another example is consulting provided by IBM under its slogan "IBM means service". Recently, I have been consulting on proposals for innovative work practices, such as working with small retailers on how to improve the customer interface using tablet terminals, as well as considering successful ways to sell system solutions.

The final approach is in the top right quadrant. It is a shift from a function-based value proposition to sensory values, while at the same time switching the value proposition method from being hard-centered to a more composite approach with various services added. This quadrant is simply the new combination of Schumpter. It is typified by the case of Apple. The structural elements that combine to create Apple's integrated business model are stylish gadgets or portable music players, communication systems, iTunes — a distribution service for music, movies and videos, iBook — a software for managing books, a diverse range of exciting applications that can be used in a variety of lifestyle situations, continually evolving Mac OS, and Apple stores that offer high-touch support for any customer queries or product problems. Adding a stylish design, music and video distribution service, and various other elements to the functional value of portable terminals or music players can be considered as a new combination model.

Apple's customer value is characterized by being fluid in the sense that even after purchasing a hard element such as a terminal, the customer can interact with Apple and create their own value through finding solutions to suit their individual lifestyle. The point here is understanding that simply creating a new combination using various elements does not bring about innovation. As seen in Apple's model, the result of focusing on customer relationships for joint value creation is realizing a cycle of further strengthening and developing these relationships, through which the company is accepted by its customers and true innovation can be achieved.

Traditionally, the schema has been that the manufacturing industry means creating goods and the service industry means providing services. However, I believe that innovation first occurs when a company is accepted by its customers. This creates feelings of happiness and appreciation for recognizing the company's efforts in creating goods. At the core of this are hard elements in the service industry, which are there because of the manufacturing industry. I believe this is how we need to view innovation.

2.2.7 *Value Chain: How to Build a System that Creates Value*

In section 2.2.6, I introduced four categories as basic patterns for creating value within marketing applications.

These are merely categories, and each industry needs to devise its own original way of value creation. Once the customer value has been decided, a value chain must be built for actually creating the value and continually strengthened while being adapted to the proposed value.

The key value chains that are fundamental in creating customer value can be summarized into three, as follows:

(1) Operation management (production/manufacturing),
(2) Customer relationship management (sales/service), and
(3) Innovation management (research/development).

Needless to say, the relative importance of each process differs considerably according to what type of customer strategy is adopted. For instance, if an innovation-seeking strategy is selected, the focus will be on the innovation control process. Conversely, if a low total cost strategy is promoted, the operation control process will be key. In either case, each process can be organically linked to support the value proposition. Subsequently, the multiple internal processes in a company are integrated and synchronized, thus raising its superiority as a system and making imitation more difficult. As a result, this superiority as a system becomes increasingly sustainable. Therefore, it is vital to coordinate and synchronize each function with marketing so as to enable the system to function organically.

I will now summarize the main points of this process.

Customer Strategy	The Focus of Internal Business Processes (Value Chain)		
	Operations Management (Production)	Customer Relationship Mgmt (Sales)	Innovation Management (R&D)
Low-Total-Cost Strategy	Highly Efficient Operation Process & Efficient, Timely Distribution	Ease of Access for Customers; Superb Post-sales Service	Seek Process Innovations & Gain Scale Economies
Product Leadership Strategy	Flexible Manufacturing Process & Rapid Introduction of New Products	Capture Customer Ideas for New Offerings & Educate Customers about Complex New Products/Services	Disciplined, High Performance Product Development and First-to-Market
Complete Customer Solutions Strategy	Deliver Broad Product/Service Line, Create Network of Suppliers for Extended Product/Service Capabilities	Create Customized Solutions for Customers, Build Strong Customer Relationships, Develop Customer Knowledge	Identify New Opportunities to Serve Customers. Anticipate Future Customer Needs
Lock-in Strategies	Provide Capacity for Proprietary Product/Service, Reliable Access and ease of Use	Create Awareness, Influence Switching Costs of Existing and Potential Customers	Develop and Enhance Proprietary Product, Increase application of Standard

Source: Adapted from Kaplan and Norton (2008).

Figure 2.67.   Building and coordinating a value chain in line with customer values.

	Production	R&D	Logistics	Technical Service
Support required for the Marketing Department	►Sales forecasts	►Market/ competitor data ►Customer needs data	►Sales forecasts ►Delivery service needs	►Customer-specific targets and plans ►Commitments to customers
Contribution to Strategy	►Production quantity, quality ►Supply speed	►New products/ technology ►Competitor Tracking	►Accurate delivery ►Traceability	►Training ►Trouble shooting

Requires coordination and synchronization with the planning activities of each department

Marketing Management

Source: Adapted from Hutt and Speh (2004).

Figure 2.68.   Marketing as a system (Cross Functional Collaboration).

2.2.8 *Organizations and Systems: How to Develop Infrastructure for Realizing Strategy*

So once the scope of business has been determined and the functional strategy for supporting the competitive and marketing strategy is clarified, a company also needs to consider its organizations and systems as infrastructure for making each strategy functional. In this section, I will discuss the McKinsey's 7S model for realizing a functional organization. Organizational reform will perhaps also be necessary for facilitating these strategies; I will comment on this point at the end of this chapter.

The 7S model demonstrates the diversity and inter-relation of several elements within corporate strategy. The elements of the 7S model do not have a start order or a rank relationship. In a company with outstanding performance, the elements complement and enhance one another, and are constantly working together towards achieving the company's goals. Basically, it's not a case of which S is more important, but rather if the 7S model can be fully leveraged overall.

The components of the 7S model are listed below:

- Shared Values (Social mission or super ordinary goals).
- Strategy (What the company tries to do to gain competitive advantages).
- Structure (Classic organization, authority relationships).
- Systems (Processes of the company, how work is done).
- Style (Culture, common way of thinking and behaving, informal rules in the organization).
- Staff (People in the company with intrinsic talents).
- Skills (Institutional and individual skills to carry out the company's strategy).

The 7S model was devised by McKinsey & Co. based on the ideas of Tom Peterson and Robert Waterman (1982). It summarizes the seven elements that mutually complement and affect each other when an organization moves to the strategy implementation stage. Taking its name from the first letter of the seven elements, the 7S model is divided in to three hard and four soft elements.

The three hard elements (3S) are strategy, structure, and systems. Here, strategy includes the scope of business and competitive, marketing, and functional strategies. Structure refers to the basic configuration of an organization, such

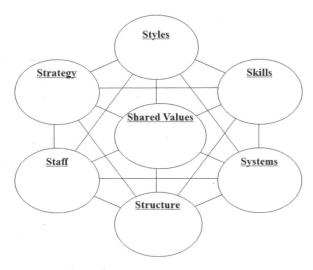

Figure 2.69.   The 7S framework: components of an organization.

as the business department system and function-specific groups. Systems are the mechanisms that run an organization, including decision making, responsibilities and authorities, information distribution, and how work is done. These three hard elements (3S) are considered relatively easy to modify.

The four soft elements (4S) are shared values, style, skills, and staff. Style is the corporate climate and culture, while skills refer to the core competences that are a combination of the unique skills and technologies an organization has. Staff are the human resources of an entire organization, and shared values are the ideals and principles recognized and shared by all staff — they could also be regarded as an organization's mission. These four soft elements (4S) are considered relatively difficult to modify. Therefore, rather than adopting a haphazard approach, an organization needs to work under a clearly defined vision and strategy when managing its own reform.

The above 7S model suggests that all of these seven elements are essential for the effective implementation of strategy.

Lastly, I will cite some key points for facilitating organizational reform, based on comments made by Behman N. Tabrizi (2007).

Points in organizational reform:

(1) Sharing and fostering a sense of crisis (carry out own present state analysis, including by staff)
(2) Building a sense of solidarity within the organization (sharing the organization's vision, holding kick-off events in which all staff participate)
(3) Branding of departments (raising internal/external recognition, image improvement, strengthening activities for increasing supporters within the organization)
(4) Developing a plan for reformation (including how to handle forces of resistance to change and how to make people get involved)
(5) Risk management (flexible response and creative approach to unforeseen events)
(6) Achieving short-term results (aiming for small successes in the relatively early stages)
(7) Measuring and evaluating progress (tracking the implementation plan and using a multifaceted evaluation that goes beyond just numerical results)
(8) Celebrations and toasts enjoyed by everyone (celebratory events for promoting communication between and within business departments)

2.3 Performance Results

In this book, strategic management as a system has been examined with a focus on the components of corporate strategy and business strategy. To finish, I would like to touch upon the importance of understanding the nature and risk of business by presenting a strategy through numbers.

Sales or profit are very important quantitative indices when discussing the results of strategic management. In truth, there is a qualitative index that is as important as sales and profits. The answer is branding. Unless a strong relationship with customers is created, a bond in other words, it is difficult to build a competitive advantage on a long-term basis. It is not enough to be able to temporarily differentiate through the functions or quality of products. In this text, I will distinguish between the quantitative elements (sales, profit) of the results of strategy and qualitative elements (branding).

2.3.1 *Understanding Brand Building*

To build a brand relationship is to create a strong bond with customers. The quality of a brand relationship can be measured by the following items:

Elements	Measuring items (examples)
Quality of the partner	This brand is attentive to my needs This brand is reliable This brand meets my interests
Connection to self (identification)	This brand is a part of me This brand expresses me This brand helps me become closer to my ideal self
Love, attachment, commitment	I love this brand I am faithful to this brand I want to maintain my relationship with this brand into the future
Intimacy (from consumers to brand)	I know the history and background of this brand I know the origin or significance of this brand I know more about this brand than other people
Intimacy (from brand to consumers)	This company understands my needs It conceptualizes products that suit me This company understands me as a person

Data: From Fournier (2009).

Figure 2.70.   Quality of brand relationship.

Brand relationship can be understood as something that moves upwardly from the base to the pinnacle in consecutive steps. Although the pinnacle signifies the bond, branding is arranged in four hierarchies, which include the top. This is called the Brand Resonance Pyramid.

(1) Quantitatively and qualitatively increasing recognition (identity): Brand awareness refers to the customer's

ability to recall or recognize a brand under different conditions.

(2) Acceptance of the meaning of the brand (specialty, class/image of usage situation): Brand meaning can be captured by examining two broad categories: (i) brand performance — the way in which the product/service meets the more functional needs of customers, and (ii) brand imagery — the ways in which the brand attempts to meet the more abstract psychological or social needs of customers.

(3) Drawing out a favorable market response (rational judgment/emotional response): As a branding strategy is implemented, special attention should be given to how customers react to the brand. Four types of customer judgments are particularly vital. They are Quality, Credibility, Consideration Set, and Superiority. Feelings refer to the emotional reactions of the customers to the brand, including warmth, fun, excitement, and security.

(4) Building a relationship and bond with customers (loyalty commitment): Brand resonance represents the strength of the psychological bond that a customer has with a brand and the degree to which this

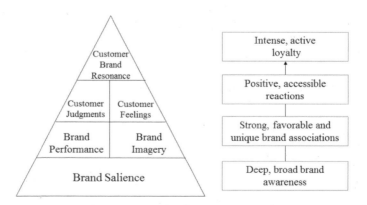

Figure 2.71. Customer-based brand equity, by Kevin Keller (2001).

connection translates into loyalty, attachment, and active engagement with the brand.

2.3.2 *Financial Projections*

In the end, business strategy comes down to numbers. Some time ago, I was invited to a presentation competition hosted by the global department of a manufacturing company. The presentation consisted of members from the global department pitching their global business strategy to their management team. They proposed very stimulating strategic options such as a market development strategy in emerging markets, a strategy of deep penetration into the niche segment of the EU market, as well as a strategy to develop new products for Africa. My role was to pose questions to the members and give summarizing comments.

The fact that it was an overseas market made it difficult to carry out present state analysis. However, by gathering secondary information through Google, etc., and conducting a focus group interview, albeit with limited interviewees, I believe they did a reasonably good job of examining the hypothesis. Passionate appeals were made to the president, and it seemed as if the presentation competition was a great success. Yet, many on the management team were not fully convinced that their proposals were going to work. Do you know why?

The reason is because the sales model and profit model, which are the finishing touches to a business model, were not included. The proposed plans were relatively clever, and the business strategy that was laid out contained some interesting ideas. However, the most important message on profitability was missing.

After the impassioned presentation, the executives would ask, "So, how much are we going to make?" It is difficult to have a discussion on the strengths and weaknesses of a strategy or its direction of improvement without a perspective on the expected sales or profit, and without knowing how much business value will be created by its implementation. Creating a temporary sales model, and examining a more promising strategic option based on it, are the reasons to utilize a sales model. Of course, it is challenging to make a sales model for a product with a new concept like Segway. Although even then, it is possible to have a discussion on the proposed hypothesis. For example, we can have a conversation on whether the initially projected business scale, exclusive to the target market, will be reached or if it will arrive at a break-even point with the said volume. Sales projections are not made to be on the mark; rather, they are the means to further improve the process by examining the strategic options.

2.4 Summary of the Key Points

When we hear feasibility evaluation, we tend to think this requires examination by utilizing our financial expertise after calculating the present value of the business. Of course, this doesn't mean that we should not use sophisticated financial engineering. However, we need to measure for consistency by first taking into account the exactness of the cash flow (CF) required for the application of financial engineering, such as present value or IRR.

How do we calculate sales? If we are looking at a market type such as general consumer products, this would most likely be done by extracting the target market from the whole, and multiplying that by shares and then doing the same with the unit price. This is probably similar to making a rough estimate of the projected fixed and variable costs, and then calculating the profit by subtracting all of that from sales.

As for a feasibility evaluation concerning business strategy, rather than being caught up with minute calculations, it is more important that the key points be covered; for the rest, it is fine to make calculations by boldly using hypotheses (we call this simulation). We can consider strategic options as a predictor variable in order to achieve the actualization of maximum future cash flow as a response variable.

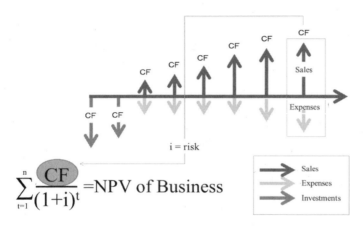

Figure 2.72.   The maximization of projected future CF.

For confirmation, I would like to check what kind of inconveniences would occur if the business strategy is not examined using sales and profit. As a rough summary, I consider that it takes the following form. Put simply, there is a great deal to lose if business strategy is not quantified.

- Unable to identify the order of priority.
- Unclear as to which solution will contribute to maximum profit.
- Limited enthusiasm among team members for implementation.
- Unclear as to how much value can be created.

So what are the important points when actually quantifying a business strategy? Basically, the focus should be on simplicity, as in the back-of-the-envelope model, with quantification based on simple simulations.

For example, it is recommended to create a model by grasping the number of customers in the target market, purchasing unit price per customer, frequency of purchasing by customers, and the cost for customer acquisition, and then conduct a simple simulation by changing the key elements or variables that compose the model. If it is not possible to get the information, you can implement an impact study by fixing other variables and changing the variables in question at a certain level.

Examples of sales models:

$$\text{Sales} = \text{number of projects} \times \text{cover rate} \times \text{winning rate} \times \text{project unit price}$$

$$\text{Sales} = \text{target market} \times \text{relative frequency (adoption rate)} \times \text{share} \times \text{price}$$

$$\text{Sales} = \text{number of distributors} \times \text{sales}$$

$$\text{Sales} = \text{market size} \times \text{share}$$

$$\text{Sales} = \text{number of users} \times \text{spending amount per customer}$$

$$\text{Sales} = \text{numbers} \times \text{unit price}$$

$$\text{Sales} = \text{sales to Toyota} + \text{sales to GM} + \text{sales to Ford}$$

To reiterate, simulation is a process of trial and error for determining a strategic option that is intended to maximize future cash flow, by linking the elements of cash flow with the components of a business strategy.

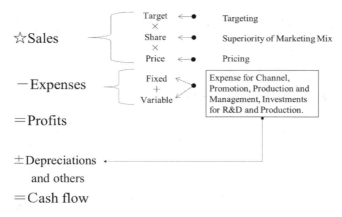

Figure 2.73.   Elements of CF/business strategy.

The steps for calculating business value as a simulations are as follows.

(1) Calculate the cash flow for every year during the growth period (forecast period)
(2) Calculate the value of the business during stable periods (terminal value)
(3) Convert the forecasted cash flows into the present value
(4) Make judgments based on the investment criteria

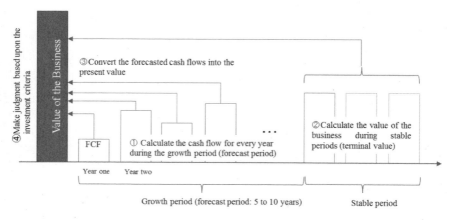

Figure 2.74.   Financial projection.

2.4.1 *Use Free Cash Flow When Calculating the Value of a Business*

This refers to the cash that can be freely used by investors, such as shareholders and creditors. Considering that this is to be cash that investors are free to use, taxes must first be subtracted. Specifically, first calculate the business revenues and then subtract corporate taxes. In reality, this is calculated by multiplying operating income by (1 − corporate tax rate). Depreciation and amortization expenses are then added to this figure. Then, subtract capital expenditures and increases in working capital. This will result in the free cash flow that is available for shareholders and creditors to use at will.

Working capital is calculated by subtracting payables from the total of inventories and trade receivables. Working capital increases as business expands because of the resulting net increase in trade receivables and inventories. An increase in inventories also means an increase in cash that must be paid. The same can be said for capital expenditures. For this reason, capital expenditures must also be subtracted. It takes time for the raw materials that are purchased to be converted into products and sold, and for the proceeds from these sales to be collected. In accounting terminology, inventory refers to goods in the stage between purchase and sales and trade receivables refer to goods in the stage between sales and collection of the sales proceeds. Meanwhile, trade payable refers to goods in the stage between purchase and payment for the goods purchased. In comparison to the period between purchase and payment, the period consisting of purchase, sales, and collection of the proceeds is longer, and cash is required to cover for this gap.

Working capital is calculated using the following formula:

$$\text{Increase in working capital} = \text{increase in trade receivables} + \text{increase in inventories} - \text{increase in trade payables}$$

Free cash flow = operating income
(1 − corporate tax rate) + depreciation
and amortization expenses − capital
expenditures − increase in working capital

2.4.2 Calculating the Value of the Business During Stable Periods

When calculating business value, it is useful to take the approach of carefully considering the expected customers, competitive environment, company environment, and macroeconomic environment in five years in the future, so as to be the base for yearly cash flows. Then the business area and target customers can be selected and assumptions made for the products to be provided, unit prices, and various expenses. It is not reasonable to make individual assumptions for sales and profits over ten years in the future for businesses subject to dramatic changes. For this reason, when estimating business value, a specific period should be set as the forecast period and the assumption made that a certain level of performance will be sustained following that. Specifically, if for example a forecast period is stipulated with five years as its final year, the business value will be calculated based on the performance in year five. So in the case of a bond that provides a set payment of 100,000 yen every year and assuming a discount rate of 5%, i would be 5%. As cash flow (CF) of 100,000 yen can be gained, then assuming a principal of X, 100,000 yen can be viewed as interest when multiplying this bond by 5%. If $X \times 5\% = 100,000$ yen, then $X = 100,000 \div 0.05 = 2,000,000$ yen. This formula can be expressed as Present Value $(PV) = CF/i$.

When converting the forecasted cash flows into the present value, the weighted average cost of capital (WACC) is used as the discount rate. This is the procurement cost calculated using the weighted average of debt costs and shareholders' equity costs by the ratio of procurement via debt and shares. The business value can be calculated by using this discount rate to find the present value of all cash flows.

Table 2.2. Financial projection.

	FY 2014
Sales	8,000
Cost of goods sold	2,400
Gross profit	5,600
Selling, general, and administrative expenses	3,200
Depreciation	280
Operating icome	2,120
Corporate taxes (35%)	742
After-tax income	1,378
Accou receivable	1,600
Inventory	240
Accout payable	480
Working capital	1,360

How should the value of the following business be calculated?
Assumptions:

(1) Forecast period of five years between 2015 and 2019,
(2) Sales grow at an annual rate of 5% for the five years between 2014 and 2019, and Free Cash Flow (FCF) grows at 2% subsequently,
(3) Cost of goods sold is 30% of sales,
(4) Selling, general, and administrative expenses are 40% of sales,
(5) Depreciation and amortization expenses for 2015: 300, 2016: 300, 2017: 320, 2018: 320, 2019: 320,
(6) Corporate tax rate: 35%,
(7) Trade receivables: 20% of sales,
(8) Inventory: 10% of cost of goods sold,
(9) Payables: 20% of cost of goods sold, and
(10) Discount rate (WACC): 10%.

	2014	2015	2016	2017	2018	2019
Sales	8,000	8,400	8,820	9,261	9,724	10,210
Cost of goods sold	2,400	2,520	2,646	2,778	2,917	3,063
Gross profit	5,600	5,880	6,174	6,483	6,807	7,147
Selling, general, and administrative expenses	3,200	3,360	3,528	3,704	3,890	4,084
Depreciation	280	300	300	˙320	320	320
Operating icome	2,120	2,220	2,346	2,458	2,597	2,743
Corporate taxes(35%)	742	777	821	860	909	960
After-tax income	1,378	1,443	1,525	1,598	1,688	1,783
Trade receivables	1,600	1,680	1,764	1,852	1,945	2,042
Inventory	240	252	265	278	292	306
Payables	480	504	529	556	583	613
Working capital	1,360	1,428	1,499	1,574	1,653	1,736
Changes in working capital		68	71	75	79	83
Capital expenditures	350	400	400	400	420	420
Operating income	2,120	2,220	2,346	2,458	2,597	2,743
Corporate taxes(35%)	742	777	821	860	909	960
After-tax income	1,378	1,443	1,525	1,598	1,688	1,783
Depreciation and ammortizations	280	300	300	320	320	320
Changes in working capital		68	71	75	79	83
Caital expenditures	350	400	400	400	420	420
Free Cash Flow (FCF)	1,308	1,275	1,354	1,443	1,509	1,600
Terminal value						20,404
FCF(total)		1,275	1,354	1,443	1,509	22,005
Present value		1,159	1,119	1,084	1,031	13,663
Present value total		18,056				

Terminal Value＝Cash flow expected in the next of the final year in the projection period ÷ (WACC—expected growth rate of FCF in the future)＝1,600 (1+0.02) ÷ (0.1-0.02)

Figure 2.75.   Spread sheet for financial projection.

Lastly, judgment is made based on the investment criteria. If the criteria are satisfied then the investment should be conducted, while the investment should not be conducted if the criteria are not satisfied.

3 Case Study

In this chapter, I will discuss a case study of a start-up manufacturer that has achieved strategically radical growth through open innovation, as a basis for applying a strategic management framework. I will feature discussion questions regarding the case, which will be presented in each step as exercises for consolidating what you've learnt so far. Chapter 3 is a summary of the contents in Chapters 1 and 2, and presents a scenario for achieving rapid growth. This case study is only an example; the real business world is continuously changing. Needless to say, in order to keep abreast of changes, you are advised to go beyond the theories and frameworks presented in this book and examine their applications in the real world.

3.1 Overview of the Case

I conducted interview-based research twice, in 2010, on growing companies that have their principal production sites in China. The research revealed typical growth patterns of Chinese contract manufacturers functioning as a receptacle for the outsourcing strategies of Japanese, European and American original equipment manufacturers (OEMs).

As outsourcing by Japanese, European and American OEMs has increased, contract manufacturers have significantly expanded their production shares, particularly in the electronics sector, by further enhancing their production process by purchasing, streamlining, and integrating the manufacturing divisions and plants that Japanese, European and American manufacturers no longer need. They are increasing their productivity by accepting orders from multiple OEMs (occasionally, and in many cases, OEMs that are actually competitors) in order to maximize economies of scale. Manufacturing operations, the majority of which are concentrated in low-cost regions such as China, have grown considerably in recent years in the electronics industry. Examples include Hon Hai Precision Industry Co., Ltd., Compal Electronics, and Winstron Corporation. These contract manufacturers specializing in electronics are collectively referred to as EMSs (abbreviation of "electronics manufacturing services," which are companies that provide contract manufacturing services for electronics manufacturers). The top management of multiple EMSs were directly interviewed during the research. Of the EMSs covered, Galanz is introduced in this report.

I focused on growth rates in selecting Galanz, which took two years to become the number one company in China and only six years to become the top selling company in the world in the production of microwave ovens. The company was producing 50% or more of the world's microwave ovens as of 2008, and has been the leading company in the Chinese market for 13 consecutive years in terms of sales. Although it was a small company that originally started out as an EMS, it is now a conglomerate with 13 subsidiaries and 52 branch offices worldwide as of the end of 2014. It also has a broad product line-up ranging from microwave ovens to refrigerators, washers, rice cookers, pots, ovens, and air conditioners, among others. I hope to first shed light on the characteristics of the growing Chinese manufacturing industry through the company's growth mechanism.

3.1.1 *History of the Company*

In 1993, Galanz contracted with Toshiba to produce OEM Toshiba-branded microwave ovens. Galanz later purchased the appliance division from Toshiba, in return for Toshiba holding a 5% stake. Production started slowly with only 10,000 microwaves produced in the first year, but expanded rapidly after that. In addition to microwave ovens, the company has recently begun producing air conditioners. Over the years, Galanz has expanded its product line to include air conditioners, washing machines, toaster ovens, refrigerators, and other home appliances. The company currently has production bases in Zhongshan City and the Shunde District of Foshan City, and employs over 50,000 people.

The pricing strategy that Galanz embraced may be pointed out as a characteristic of the company's growth mechanism. Galanz reduced the prices of its microwave ovens nine times during the period from 1996 through 2003. The level of reduction was astounding, averaging between 30% to 40%. When its production of microwave ovens reached one million units, Galanz set its selling prices at levels lower than the manufacturing costs of its competitors (production volume of 500 thousand units). Further, when its production volume reached 10 million units, the company set the selling prices at levels lower than the manufacturing costs of a competitor manufacturing five million units.

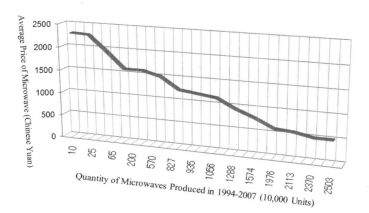

Source: Based on internal material.

Figure 3.1. Extremely intense price competition and expansion of production capacity.

The logic underlying the pricing policy described above is as follows: First, introduce advanced technologies by functioning as an outsourcing receptacle for OEMs. Rather than take advantage of the OEMs solely as providers of advanced technologies, secure orders from them to use as a buffer and expand production capacity. In order to ensure that expanded capacity is used, regularly carry out disruptive price markdowns as described above; thereby expanding the lower- to middle-class market segment itself, along with the company's share within the segment. This is a so-called cost leadership strategy.

Additionally, the company has been setting forth measures for enhancing the vertical integration of its value chain in recent years. Specifically, it is investing aggressively in strengthening its research and development functions, as well as in the Galanz brand itself. It is believed that this signifies the company's implementation of a differentiation strategy. It can also be construed as an attempt to strike a balance within a very short period between its cost leadership strategy and its differentiation strategy, which are on opposing ends of the spectrum and are believed to be statically incompatible. What renders this possible is open innovation.

In contrast to the innovation of Japanese companies, which is highly likely to take place in-house in a closed environment, the innovation model of Galanz may be considered open. The aforementioned evolution of Galanz is also backed by the company's visions consisting mainly of: (a) moving from "the world's plant" to "global brand," (b) moving from "made in China" to "created in China," and (c) global layout of R&D.

3.2 Innovation of EMS

The strategies of EMSs, including Galanz, are generally to reduce prices in order to increase sales based upon price competitiveness. The companies are strongly aware of the logic of ultimately being able to increase profit, even if prices are low, by reducing the production cost per unit by achieving greater production volumes than their competitors.

Galanz and other EMSs have the following points in common, in terms of their evolution:

- Acquisition of technologies from OEM clients (reduction of development costs)
- Specialized product concepts incorporating minimum necessary functions (cost reduction through the simplification of design)
- Establishing large-scale production systems (economies of scale)
- Hiring skilled workers from advanced competitors (experience curve effects, reduction of education and training costs), selecting locations contributing to lower production costs (reduction of fixed costs)
- Open and modular architecture (reduction of production cost)

This strategy is based on the so-called economies of scale, which involves expanding production scales in order to reduce the cost per unit by distributing the fixed costs across a large volume of products. However, it should be remembered that the experience curve effect of a "decrease in production costs with an increase in cumulative production volume" is also at work. It signifies the idea that years of continuous learning within a single industry leads to increased work efficiency. The effect that learning has on reducing the cost of production is attributable not only to the efficiency of individual line workers, but also to the acquisition of knowledge and skills for improving team work and designing production processes. The experience curve effect also applies to economic activities outside of production, inducing distribution, R&D, and marketing (Saloner, Shepard and Podolny, 2001).

A fact that is believed to be of extreme importance is that, despite popular belief that advantages such as economic efficiency and strong appeal to consumers work to the benefit of existing companies, Galanz, a late comer, was the one that benefited from these advantages in driving out the existing companies. According to *The Innovator's Dilemma* by Christensen (1997), sustaining technological progress exceeds the performance level required by the market at times, resulting in an opportunity for disruptive technology in the low-end market segment. In essence, Galanz's strategy described above may also be perceived as disruptive innovation by a low-cost modular manufacturer in areas where advanced companies have fallen into an innovation dilemma.

To use a Schumpeterian expression, the series of measures implemented by Galanz are none other than concentrated embodiments of a "new combination" for reducing costs. Schumpeter (1926) lists the five types of new combinations as: introducing a new product, opening a new market, introducing a new method of production, acquiring a new source of raw materials, and introducing a new organizational form. Galanz realized a new experience curve by providing products based on new concepts, which specifically perform the minimum necessary functions, to mid-range markets in developing regions using new methods of production, including the utilization of advanced outside companies. Viewing the rapid progress that Chinese EMSs are making simply in terms of IP infringement issues would be to lose sight of the nature of the matter.

Although many EMSs start out as a so-called *shan zhai* (imitation product manufacturers), they eventually begin to supply products sold under the private labels of European and American mass retailers as they acquire production technologies. They may also begin supplying their own house-label products based on their proprietary intellectual properties as qualified brand-name manufacturers. Galanz has already moved on to this new stage.

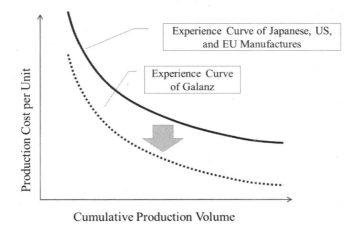

Figure 3.2. Galanz's experience curve based on a "new combination".

3.3 Japanese "Monozukuri" (Shop-floor Production) Culture and Digitalization

I hope to give consideration to the future direction of the Japanese manufacturing industry, which built its brands based on *monozukuri* or shop-floor-production. First, the Japanese manufacturing industry and its surrounding environmental factors will be examined. The following may be pointed out as the characteristics of the Japanese manufacturing industry. In fact, Japanese companies have achieved overwhelmingly strong positions in a domain comprised largely of mechanical analogue elements, such as automobiles, machinery, precision equipment, and office equipment, by strengthening and utilizing the aforementioned elements as their competence in order to establish competitive superiority within the domain.

- Corporate culture of field-oriented *monozukuri*.
- Cooperative relationship between the primary product manufacturer (OEM) and its subcontracting plants, which supports this corporate culture.
- Technology for achieving diverse and sophisticated functions through hardware (component) integration.

- Vertically integrated companies with extensive in-house technology (mass of implicit knowledge).
- Essentially the highest QCDS (Quality, Cost, Delivery, and Service) in the world.

However, a new and prominent trend of digitalization has been sweeping towards the Japanese manufacturing industry in recent years. Digitalization in the manufacturing industry signifies the replacement of physical integration indispensable to *monozukuri* with operations employing semiconductor chips and microprocessors (microcomputers) for controlling the chips. It is also a fact that, in reality, the number of custom-made hardware components requiring high levels of adaptation, which Japanese manufacturers excel in, is decreasing as modular products with an internal structure consisting of a combination of highly versatile hardware components and sophisticated software are developed. As a result, Japanese companies are no longer able to generate sufficiently high added value in terms of hardware production, in spite of their advanced integration technologies.

Another impact is the possible provision by Galanz and other EMSs of low-end to mid-range products in domains where Japanese companies have had an advantage over others in terms of providing high-end products; namely, the Japanese, USA, and EU markets, which are considered upper class from a global perspective.

The strategic directionality frequently suggested by Japanese corporate managers, as a result of their analysis of this situation, is specialization in businesses that only Japanese companies are capable of handling. It involves the decision to focus on custom-made and high-end products that require high levels of integration for production, and abandon the low-end and mid-range segments.

Investing resources in domains where competitive superiority cannot be expected certainly is not advisable as a short-term strategy. From a long-term perspective, however, many point out that the strategy of not covering the mid-range segment may result in the loss of major growth potential. The middle class in emerging regions is significant. In the case of China, for example, the class of people with a disposable annual income of US $5,000 or higher but less than US $35,000 accounts for 33.4% of the Chinese population, or 443.56 million people. It may indeed be said that the "one who wins in the Chinese middle-class market wins the global market" (Jin, 2010).

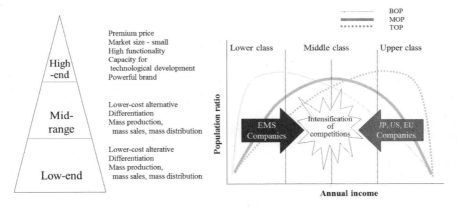

Figure 3.3. Business development of local EMS companies the Chinese market.

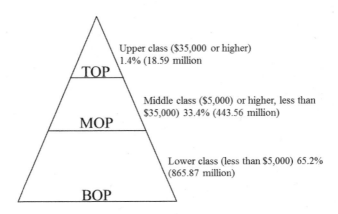

Source: Euromonitor International, China Annual Statistics 2009.
Data: Figures are the annual disposal income per household.

Figure 3.4. Emerging Chinese middle class market.

3.4 Competitive Strategy: Benefits to Offer and Forms to Deliver Benefits

Finally, I propose a number of conceivable basic competitive strategies for Japanese manufacturers. The strategy types are based on the customer benefits delivered and the forms to deliver them.

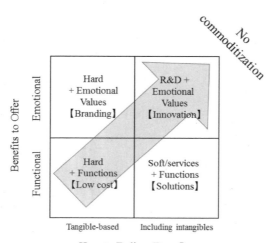

How to Deliver Benefits

Source: Adapted from Naryandes (2003) and Nobeoka (2006).

Figure 3.5.   Strategy types based on benefits delivered and form of delivery.

First, the lower left quadrant represents the strategy of delivering economic benefits based mainly on hardware. This is the strategy of developing products with basic functionality for the aforementioned middle class by eliminating excessive functions and providing products at price levels that allow companies to benefit from high cost performance. The key here is that "low price" does not necessarily signify "low quality." In order for companies to succeed in this domain, they must carefully note the innovator's dilemma (Christensen, 1997) that "sustaining technological progress exceeds the performance level required by the market at times, creating opportunities for low-end technologies that subsequently results in dramatic changes in the market." It is necessary to understand the performance level that customers expect so that "required performance = actual performance."

So, what are the factors that define the performance level that customers expect? The two factors involved are the customer's "understanding of the product," — which is the ability to determine the significance of relevant performance levels — and the customer's "involvement". Ikeo (2010) states that while high involvement does not necessarily signify a requirement for high performance levels, "involvement" tends to be high for applications requiring higher performance levels. In order to compete with EMSs and other manufacturers based in developing regions, companies are expected to lower prices strategically by making sharp distinctions among parts that should be manufactured in-house, those that should be outsourced to business partners, and those that should be purchased from outside suppliers. This is not limited to manufacturing. The localization of a "new combination," i.e. innovation, is indispensable, including low-cost local distribution, utilization of sales channels, local procurement of materials, raw material and facilities, and localized development.

One approach in the upper left quadrant is promoting sensory values. This refers to demonstrating a product's sensory values of stimulus to the five senses such as usability and design, and also a global perspective, warmth and excitement. In PC products, this is illustrated in Panasonic's Toughbook® and Toughpad® products. As the name suggests, these are durable products that can function well in any type of tough environment, thus providing peace of mind to the target customers of construction workers, police and special brigades. The point of this quadrant is branding a product as a hard element.

The solution quadrant in the lower right also takes the approach of providing a direct solution to the customer by adding software, such as consulting and other services, to the hardware, which is the product, instead of providing only the hardware. For example, this is the approach where, when providing a mission critical system, consulting services precede the provision of a total solution package consisting of software, hardware, middleware, and applications. A good example of this is reform of the business model by Louis Gerstner of IBM, in which he established the concept of a customer-oriented total solution provider. Garsner communicated this message clearly to those inside and outside the company using the phrase "IBM means service." At the same time, on the business side, he acquired consulting firms, as well as built a model involving the integrated provision of the optimum combination of solutions for the customer, which included external procurement of peripheral hardware and applications, while adhering to in-house products for core hardware and middleware to integrate the various applications.

The last quadrant is the domain of innovation in the upper right. It is a shift from a function-based value proposition to emotional values, while at the same time switching the value proposition method from being hard oriented to a more composite approach with various services added. This quadrant is simply the new combination of Schumpter, and is typified by Apple. The structural elements that combine to create Apple's integrated business model are stylish gadgets or portable music players, communication systems, iTunes — a distribution service for music, movies and videos, iBook — a software for managing books, a diverse range of exciting applications that can be used in a variety of lifestyle situations, continually evolving Mac OS, and Apple stores that offer high-tech support for any customer queries or product problems. Adding a stylish design, music and video distribution service and various other elements to the functional value of portable terminals and music players can be considered as a new combination model.

Most EMS companies begin in the lower-left quadrant and some have already moved to the left-upper quadrant. How should manufacturers, who have been successful based on high quality products with a *monozukuri* culture, respond to the dynamic development of EMSs? It is obvious that paying attention only to QCDS is not enough.

3.5 Practical Exercises

We have already shared quite a few frameworks and theories that are useful in strategic management in the previous chapters. Please pick up some, that you think are appropriate for answering the questions below and try to apply them to the case study in this chapter.

Exercise 1: Check the message stated on the web site of Galanz, and try to clarify their mission.

Exercise 2: Check the web site of a few suppliers who you think could be competitors for Galanz, such a Panasonic/Matsushita, and review their future directions according to the competitor analysis framework.

Exercise 3: Enumerate the five forces that are assumed to have an impact or influence over the industry, and clarify how they may influence Galanz in the future.

Exercise 4: Based upon the information regarding Galanz in Section 3.1, describe their core competences and value chain.

Exercise 5: Point out the main key factors for success (KFS) that explain Galanz's rapid growth by comparing the value chain of Galanz with that of one of the manufacturers you selected in Exercise 2.

Exercise 6: Clarify how the key buying factors (KBF) in emerging countries are different from those in developed countries.

Exercise 7: Using the product market growth matrix, clarify how Galanz has expanded the scope of business since its establishment up to now.

Exercise 8: Based upon the basic SWOT analysis as a summary of the 4Cs analysis, make recommendations regarding the future direction/s and strategic options in each direction for Galanz to take.

Exercise 9: Check a couple of articles regarding IoT or Internet of Things and consider what will happen in the household electronics industry in the near future.

Exercise 10: Supposing you were a person in charge of the microwave business of Matsushita, summarize the SWOT of Matsushita, and make recommendations regarding the strategic directions to pursue in the future.

4 Creating Presentation Material

In this book, I have discussed themes such as corporate strategies, business strategies which constitute corporate strategies, marketing, and functional strategies which are closely related to business strategies, and organizations and structures which support these various types of strategies, by focusing on key points as if I were lecturing at a business school or company training or explaining at a consulting conference. How did you find it so far?

Below is an explanation of the key points on creating presentation materials in the finishing process of formulating strategies.

(1) Devise a business strategy proposal by combining strategic options determined as effective for achieving business goals. Refer to Figure 4.1.

(2) Create a scenario of the business strategy proposal using the verbal model and diagram model. At the same time, list up hypotheses included in the scenario to understand business uncertainties. Refer to Figures 4.2 and 4.3.

(3) Revise the business strategy proposal using the pyramid structure and complete it as a business plan. Refer to Figures 4.4 and 4.5.

(4) Create an executive summary based on the business plan. Refer to Figure 4.6.

4.1 Combine the Strategic Elements Effective for Achieving the Business Goals

A business strategy proposal is created by combining strategic issues and options, effective for resolving each issue.

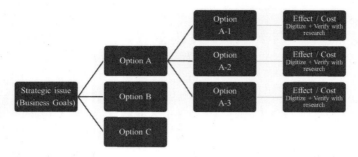

Figure 4.1. Extracting strategic options determined as effective for achieving goals.

Sales, profits and shares can be considered as strategic issues. Scope of business, competitive strategy, targeting, positioning, marketing mix or 4Ps, functional strategies, structure and system can be strategic options. The items and key points of the business strategy proposal are as follows:

(1) Business overview (vision)

Simply define the vision of what your company wants to achieve with this business and the ideal condition of the business based on the corporate mission and goals clearly defined in the corporate strategy.

(2) Situation analysis (customers, competitors, company, and context)

Set the scope of customers (markets), competitors (rival companies), and context (macro environment) for SWOT analysis, and closely examine how they will change from present to future, including your company (own resources). Simply describe the elements that are important for proposing orientation.

(3) Basic direction

  (i) Goals (SMART — sales, profits, shares, etc.) is the key.

  (ii) Scope of business (product-market growth matrix). Select the scope of business to achieve goals. The scope of business is often defined by products and markets, but it should be noted that how this business is defined directly determines the growth potential of the business. Clearly defining the scope of business is a major key theme that has strong impact on the competitive strategy and marketing management. It is important to think about this thoroughly and without compromise.

(4) Strategies

   (i) Competitive strategy (disciplines for creating value).

This is a statement of how your company will fight and win against competitors within the scope of business to achieve goals. Clearly define the basic direction of whether to increase the Willingness To Pay (WTP, or the value to customers) over that of average companies, or to maintain the WTP but lower production costs to provide products at a relatively low selling price.

   (ii) Marketing management (STP + 4Ps)

Within the selected scope of business, carefully select the specific customer market and thoroughly think about your company's unique solutions for the customer's unmet needs. Then, express these on a positioning map and develop the 4Ps. This will link directly to the sales model. An uncertain scenario will not link to the sales model.

   (iii) Functional strategy (VC)

Review research and development, production and manufacturing, management and sales, quality control, distribution, etc. This will link mainly to the cost model.

(5) Structure and systems

This is the last item but is extremely important. Describe the key points of the structure and system, including your leadership, that are necessary as infrastructures to promote all measures.

4.2 Create a Scenario and List up Hypotheses Included in It

The business strategy proposal is made into a scenario using the verbal model and diagram model.

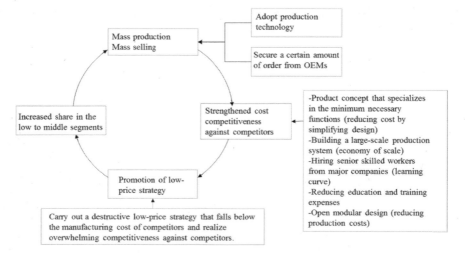

Figure 4.2.   Scenario (diagram model).

Original equipment manufacturers (OEMs) in Japan and EU have been working to improve efficiency by outsourcing production, resulting in unnecessary factories and manufacturing sectors. Our company's strategy is to purchase and utilize secondhand production facilities from such end product manufactures in Japan and EU and to aim for a sizable increase in production share as a contract manufacturer (i.e. EMS).

By functioning as the outsourcing basis for OEMs, we can secure a certain amount of orders while expecting a high growth in the global market. In addition, we will provide our private label products which are highly cost-effective, targeting the middle and lower class market segments which are not covered by OEMs and have strong potential needs. By doing so, we will contribute to the growth of these segments and at the same time we will aim to expand our share within the segments. Cost reduction measures are as follows:

- Product concept that specializes in the minimum necessary functions (reducing costs by simplifying design)
- Building a large-scale production system (economy of scale)

- Hiring senior skilled workers from major companies (experience curve)
- Reducing education and training expenses
- Open modular design (reducing production costs)

Finally, we will carry out a disruptive low-price strategy based on the above grounds and realize overwhelming competitiveness against competitors.

(Excerpted and summarized from Kasahara, 2011)

In the strategy planning stage, the business strategy proposal will include some sort of hypotheses. As strategies that contain many hypotheses will naturally bear many risks, you need to clarify as to how much verification is needed upon implementing the strategies. Prior to implementing the business strategies, plans must be made on how the individual hypothesis will be converted into knowledge. Examples of such methods include focus group interviews, in-depth interviews, surveys, and secondary research.

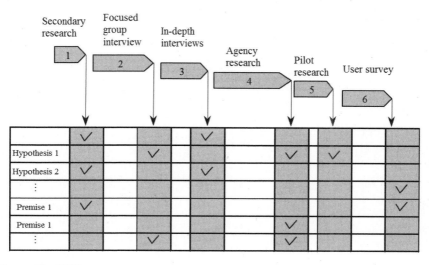

Source: Ohe (1998).

Figure 4.3.   Listing up hypotheses included in the scenario.

4.3 Revise the Scenario Using the Pyramid Structure — Express with Three Blocks: Why, What, and How

The business strategy proposal is revised using the pyramid structure and completed as a business plan. More often than not, what appears to be a business plan actually turns out to be a report with quite a different idea. There are three elements required in business strategy reports. The first is "Why?". Why does your company need to implement this strategy? The second is "What?". What should actually be done? The last of the three is "How?". How should the strategy be developed specifically?

Here is a list of some typical reports:

- An array of analysis templates (a collection of analysis tools for analysts to utilize as in value chain, Five Forces Analysis, and SWOT analysis).
- Sales and expense simulation (a description explaining how much sales will be achieved by a certain date and how much expense will be necessary in order to do so).
- The department's statement of commitment (reports that are bursting in spirit as in I'll work hard to achieve the goal! You can count on me!).

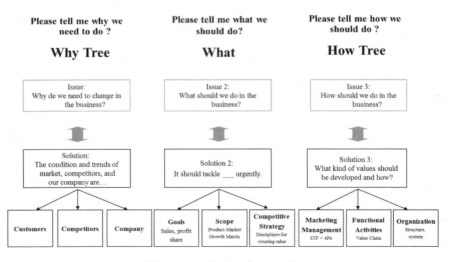

Figure 4.4. Report framework.

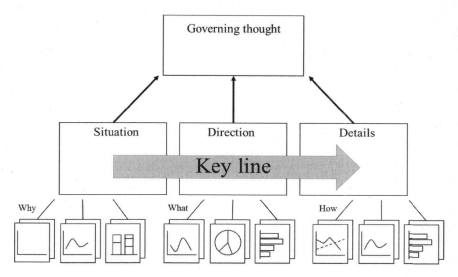

Figure 4.5. Combination of analysis and proposals.

- Cartoons reminiscent of those by the Ministry of Economy, Trade and Industry or research institutions (expressing motives using appealing illustrations, as if that would function as a strategy…).

4.4 Narrow Down the Key Points and Create a Summary

The final step is to create an executive summary based on the business plan by narrowing down the key points. If there are multiple business strategy proposals, you should select a specific business strategy proposal by weighing them against each other.

Various methods can be used for assessing proposals from considering the advantages and disadvantages of the respective proposals, to assessing quantitatively from the two perspectives of market attractiveness (the degree in terms of market size, growth potential, and competitive situation) and your company's resource fit (the degree in which your company can utilize its R&D capabilities, production capacities, and selling power in the target business).

When clear results cannot be obtained even with quantitative assessment, decisions should be made based on which proposal suits the management philosophy, and financial return. In general, the bases for assessment are:

- Advantages and disadvantages.
- Market attractiveness and resource fit.
- Risk and return.
- Effect and cost.
- Quantitative assessment (economic performance), qualitative assessment (awareness, brand power, relationship, etc.)

The final deciding factors are values (philosophy) and numbers (sales and profit).

4.5 Points in Presentation: Simple, Logical and Passionate

Lastly, when making a report using PowerPoint, I would like to recommend that you express your points by combining powerful charts and comments rather than only using text.

In marketing, there are concepts of perceived quality and perceived value. The same goes for business plans. No matter how good the content of your proposals are, they have no value if they are not perceived as attractive and worthy of consideration. Presentations must be made easy to understand even if their contents are complex and advanced. This is the secret to good presentations.

Vision	Become a global brand from being a factory for the world.
Situation analysis	In newly emerging countries, the middle segment pursuing quality of life is expected to expand rapidly. The need for good-quality home appliances in the affordable price range is increasing globally. Manufacturers in advanced countries are over-engineering in general. Our company's strengths are production technologies developed as an EMS and cost competitiveness.
Goal	Top world share in the middle range home appliances market.
Scope of business	Global development of highly cost-effective home appliances in a wide product lineup
Competitive strategy	Cost leadership strategy in a large market based on mass production and mass selling
Marketing management	Provide good-quality home appliances in the affordable price range targeting the middle class segment of newly emerging countries. Develop a full set of home appliances such as microwave ovens, rice cookers, refrigerators, washing machines, and air conditioning. By setting the selling price which falls below the competitors' cost price, we will carry out a destructive pricing policy and aim for world's top share. Customer reach will be maximized by using e-commerce as the channel.
Operational activities	Product concept that specializes in the minimum necessary functions (reducing cost by simplifying design); building a large-scale production system; hiring senior skilled workers from major companies (experience curve effect); reducing education and training expenses; open modular design; production locations consolidated in China; research and development locations selected based on their theme.
Organizations and structures:	Top-down structure by placing importance on the consistency and uniformity of the global brand.

Figure 4.6.   Example of an executive summary.

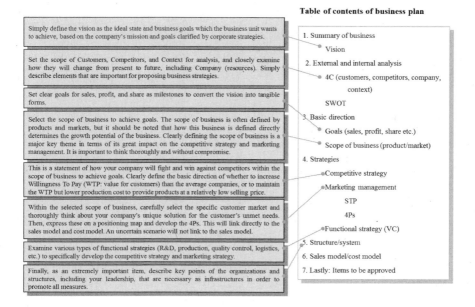

Figure 4.7.   Business plan check points.

References and Further Reading

Aaker, D. A. (2005), *Strategic Market Management*, John Wiley & Sons, Inc.

Aaker, D. A. (2013), *Strategic Market Management*, John Wiley & Sons, Inc.

Abell, D. F. (1980), *Defining the Business: The Starting Point of Strategic Planning,* Prentice Hall.

Anzoff, H. I. (1968), *Corporate Strategy*, McGraw-Hill.

Arndt, J. (1979), "Toward a Concept of Domesticated Market," *Journal of Marketing*, 43(4), 69–75.

Chernev, A. (2009), *Strategic Marketing Management*, Brightstar Media, Inc.

Christensen, C. M. (1997), *The Innovator's Dilemma*, Harvard Business School Press.

D'aveni, R.A. and Gunther, R. E. (1994), *Hypercompetition: Managing the dynamics of strategic maneuvering*, The Free Press.

Dolan, R. J. (1997), "Note on Marketing Strategy," Harvard Business School Background Note 598-061, October 1997.

Douglas, S.P. and Craig, C.S. (1983), *International Marketing Research*, Englewood Cliffs, NJ: Prentice-Hall

Freiberg, K. and Freiberg, J. (1996), *Nuts!*, Broadway Books.

Garth S., Andrea S. and Joel P. (2001), *Strategic Management,* John Wiley & Sons, Inc.

Hawkins D. and Mothersbaugh D. (2013), *Consumer Behavior: Building Marketing Strategy,* McGraw-Hill Irwin.

Hofer, C. W. and Schendel, D. (1978), *Strategy Formulation: Analytical Concepts*, West Publishing Co.

Jin, J. (2010), "Winning in the Chinese middle-class market with integrated strategy for its upper-class market," *Nihon Keizai Shimbun* (Japanese newspaper) February 22.

Kaplan, R. S. and Norton, D. P. (2008), *Converting Intangible Assets into Tangible Outcomes*, Harvard Business School Publishing

Kasahara, E. (2011), "Japanese Manufacturing Industry in the Age of Competition with Companies Located in Newly Emerging China and Taiwan: In search of new competitive strategy network," *Rikkyo DBA Journal*, 1

Kasahara, E. (2013), *Building a Strong Company: How to Apply Strategic Management for Business* , Chukei, Tokyo.

Kasahara, E., Fukuda, M. and Teraishi, M. (2000), *Venture Creation Dynamics: The Management, Evaluation, and Training Viewpoint.* Chapters 5, 6, 10, and 11 (Awarded a Small Business Research Incentive Award.) Bunshindo, Tokyo.

Keller, K. L. (2007), *Strategic Brand Management: Building Measuring and Managing Brand Eauity*, Prentice Hall.

Kotler, P. (2000), *Marketing Management (11th Ed.)*, Prentice Hall International Editions.

Kotler, P., Kartajaya, H. and Huan, H. D. (2006), *Think ASEAN! Rethinking Marketing toward ASEAN Community 2015*, McGraw-Hill Education.

Kotabe, M. and Helsen, K. (2010), *Global Marketing Management*, John Wiley & Sons.

Lodish L. M., Morgan H. L. and Kallianpur A. (2001), *Entrepreneurial Marketing*, John Wiley & Sons, Inc.

Hutt, M. D. and Speh, T. W. (2004), *Business Marketing Management: A Strategic View of Industrial and Organizational Markets,* South-Western.

Mintzberg, H., Ahlstrand, B., and Lampel, J. (1998), *Strategy Safari: A Guide Tour through the Wilds of Strategy Management,* The Free Press.

Moore, G. A. (2004), *Inside the Tornado,* Collins Business Essentials.

Morgan, R. M. and Shelby D. H. (1994), "The Commitment-Trust Theory of Relationship Marketing," *Journal of Marketing*, 58(7), 20–23.

Narayandas, D. (1995), "Long-Term Manufacturer-Supplier Relationships: Do They Pay Off for Supplier Firms?" *Journal of Marketing* 59(1), 1–16.

Narayandas, D. (2003), "Customer Management Strategy in Business Markets," Harvard Business School Working Paper #N9-503-060.

Ohe, T. (1998), *Naze Shinjigyou-wa Seikou Shinainoka* [Why Corporate Ventures Fail], Nikkei Inc.

Peters, T. and Waterman, R. (1982), *In Search of Excellence: Lesson from America's Best-Run Companies*, Sage Publication, Inc.

Prahalad, C.K. and Hamel, G. (1990), "The Core Competence of the Corporation," *Harvard Business Review*, May-June.

Schumpeter, J.A. (1926), *Theorie der wirthschaftlichen Entwicklung* [Theory of Economic Development], Duncker & Humbolt.

Shimaguchi, M. (2000), *Marketing Paradigm*, Yuhikaku Publishing Co., Ltd.

Tabrizi, B. N. (2007), *Rapid Transformation: A 90-day Plan for Fast and Effective change*, Harvard Business School Press.

Tichy, N.M and Sherman, S. (1993), *Control Your Destiny or Someone Else Will*, New York City: Doubleday.